When I Need You

A personal anthology
of favourite Christian writings

Mary Batchelor

Pickering & Inglis
LONDON · GLASGOW

Acknowledgments

The author and publishers wish to thank the following for permission to include the copyright material listed below:

Hodder & Stoughton Ltd for extracts from *The Ring of Truth* by J B Phillips; *The Imitation of Christ* by Thomas à Kempis as translated by E M Blaiklock; *Who Walk Alone* by Margaret Evening; *A Private House of Prayer* by Leslie Weatherhead; *The Hiding Place* by Corrie Ten Boom; *A Severe Mercy* by Sheldon Vanauken; and *Lord Let Me Love* by Marjorie Holmes.

Sidgwick & Jackson Ltd for poem 'The Conversion of Saul Kane' from *The Everlasting Mercy* by John Masefield.

The Saint Andrew Press for extract from *The Daily Study Bible* by William Barclay.

Collins Publishers for extracts from *Christian Behaviour, Reflections on the Psalms, The Problem of Pain*, and 'George Macdonald' — *An Anthology* by C S Lewis; *Prayers for Busy People* and *When My Visitors Go* by Rita Snowden; and *So You're Lonely* by Roy Trevivian.

Gill and Macmillan Ltd for extracts from *Prayers of Life* and *The Christian Response* by Michel Quoist; and *God is For Real, Man* by Carl Burke.

The Banner of Truth Trust for extract from *Select Letters* by John Newton.

The SCM Press Ltd for extracts from *Letters and Papers from Prison* by Dietrich Bonhoeffer; and *Interpreting the Parables* by A M Hunter.

Church Pastoral Aid Society for extracts from *A New Happiness* by Gavin Reid.

Rev. R H L Williams for prayer from *God Thoughts*.

Tyndale House Publishers for extract from *Let Me Be A Woman* by Elisabeth Elliot.

Mayhew McCrimmon Publishers for extracts from *Prayers from a Mother's Heart* by Judith Mattison.

Scripture Union for use of poems 'Question' by Mig Holder and 'Peter' by Mary Chandler from *Making Eden Grow*; extracts from *Without Jeff* by Jenny Chadwick; and *The Last Thing We Talk About* by Joseph Bayly.

Macmillan Publishers Ltd for extract from *Readings from St. John's Gospel* by William Temple.

Robson Books Limited for poems from *You Have a Minute, Lord?* by David Kossoff.

Stainer & Bell Ltd for the poem 'Lord look upon our working day' by Ian M Fraser from *Partners in Praise,* copyright 1969.

Inter-Varsity Press for extracts from *From Fear to Faith* by Martyn Lloyd-Jones; *Pages from God's Casebook* by John Hercus; and *Parents in Pain* by John White.

Marshall, Morgan & Scott for extracts from *Breakout* by Fred Lemon with Gladys Knowlton; and *The Blessings of Illness* by Basilea Schlink.

Black and white illustrations and colour cover — copyright Peter Baker — International Photobank.

Days

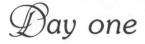
Day one

Mary has chosen what is better, and it will not be taken away from her.

Luke 10:42 NIV

How many times have you listened to an address on Martha and Mary? Perhaps the speaker was a woman, obviously in sympathy with the distracted Martha or a man, pontificating where he has little first hand experience of cooking a dinner. We end up feeling a bit sore on the subject and mystified by our Lord's approach.

Far from failing to understand the dilemma, I think that the Lord was wanting to release Martha from the level of living she had grown up to expect for herself as a woman. Often we need to be rescued too. We hear a great deal in the world at large about female equality and are not sure what the Christian reaction should be. Yet since the coming of Christ, women's equality with men has been believed and taught — at least in theory. Of course, when Women's Lib. say 'equal' they often mean 'identical' — in all but biological function. The New Testament does *not* teach the identity of the sexes for our roles and excellences very often differ from those of men. Yet in all his encounters with women our Lord was at pains to treat them as men's equals in spiritual value and capacity.

Such a concept was new to the Jews of the day. For them, Rabbinical study was forbidden for women. Yet Mary 'sat at Jesus' feet' — in the parlance of the day she took up the position of a disciple to a Rabbi. Paul, in a similar phrase, describes himself as being brought up 'at the feet of Gamaliel' when he studied under that great Rabbi. Jesus might have been expected gently but firmly to send Mary back to the kitchen, yet he refused to do so in spite of Martha's requests. For him, women, as much as men, had their place as his disciples.

Even today we have not learned the lesson. Many of us, like Martha, disapprove of a woman whose priorities put spiritual thinking and development before tidy cupboards and cordon bleu menus. To be honest, we find it easier to take refuge in baking a cake than in spiritual exercises. But Christ has called us to spiritual liberation. However much time we may have to spend on necessary household duties we must not build our own bars. As 'joint heirs' let us take possession of our spiritual inheritance.

O Love Divine, how sweet thou art!
When shall I find my willing heart
All taken up by thee?
I thirst, I faint, I die to prove
The greatness of redeeming love,
The love of Christ to me.

God only knows the love of God:
O that it now were shed abroad
In this poor stony heart!
For love I sigh, for love I pine:
This only portion, Lord, be mine,
Be mine this better part!

O that I could for ever sit
With Mary at the Master's feet!
Be this my happy choice:
My only care, delight and bliss,
My joy, my heaven on earth, be this,
To hear the Bridegroom's voice.

Charles Wesley 1707-88

Lord help me today to put first things first. Free me from the treadmill of household and business duties that would hinder me from seeking your company. I want to learn from you in the quiet of your presence so that I may go refreshed and recreated to pursue the day's work. Teach me that I am not wasting time by being still but help me to prize and value such moments above everything else. Jesus, my Lord, I love you and worship you.   Amen.

Day two

Confident of this, that he who began a good work in you will carry it on to completion until the day of Jesus Christ.

Philippians 1:6 NIV

How far removed from the idea of the New Testament are the insipid words of the hymn which says 'he came sweet influence to impart, a gracious willing guest', and goes on to say, 'and his that gentle voice we hear soft as the breath of even, that checks each fault, that calms each fear . . .' Anyone who has any experience at all of the living God knows that he is nothing at all like this somebody who tut-tuts politely at our failings and lays a soothing hand upon our anxious little heads. The God who lives in us if we allow him, is not necessarily always gentle: he can be wind and fire and a whole lot of other things. He can give us strength, but he can also show us our weakness! He will 'increase our faith', but frequently not in the way we want or expect. He will show us, as we can bear it, more and more truth, but he will shatter our illusions without scruple, perhaps especially illusions about ourselves. He will give us moments of wonderful perception, but he will also allow us to endure terrifying darkness. His dealings with us are not some optional religious game; he is in deadly earnest and he is intent on 'bringing many sons to glory'. He is indeed all goodness and light but he will show no more compunction towards the evil things that we have allowed to grow in our hearts than a human surgeon would to a malignant growth. The men of old were hardly exaggerating when they said, 'Our God is a consuming fire.'

J B Phillips   Ring of Truth

Batter my heart, three-person'd God; for, you
As yet but knock, breathe, shine, and seek to mend;
That I may rise, and stand, o'erthrow me, and bend
Your force, to break, blow, burn and make me new.
I, like an usurped town, to another due,
Labour to admit you, but O, to no end.
Reason, your viceroy in me, me should defend,
But is captiv'd, and proves weak or untrue.
Yet dearly I love you, and would be loved fain,
But am betroth'd unto your enemy:
Divorce me, untie, or break that knot again,
Take me to you, imprison me, for I
Except you enthrall me, never shall be free,
Nor ever chaste, except you ravish me.

John Donne 1572-1631

Lord, it is a fearful thing to fall into the hands of the living God. Yet, like David, I would rather fall into the hand of the Lord than into the hand of men — for your mercy is great.
Come into my life today. Cleanse my secret thoughts and desires. Deal with my deepest needs. Renew me and remake me at whatever cost until you begin to see in me the image of your dear Son. For his sake. Amen.

Day three

Submit yourselves to one another because of your reverence for Christ. Wives, submit to your husbands as to the Lord.

Ephesians 5:21-22 TEV

Rebekah, with all her beauty, and with all her courage, and with all her ambition to be in the covenant line, lacked the best thing in a woman, covenant line or no — womanly sensibility, tenderness, quietness, humility, and self-submission. And, though that speck on her heart was so small as to be wholly invisible as long as she was still a maid, and a bride, and a young wife, yet it was there. And by the time that Rebekah became no longer a bride or a young wife, this speck had spread till both her heart and her character had wholly lost all wholesomeness, and sweetness, and strength. 'The one thing certain about a wife is that the result is different from the expectation — that is, if there were ever any particular and defined expectations at all. Age, illness, an increasing family, no family at all, household cares, want of means, isolation, incompatible prejudices, quarrels, social difficulties, all tell on the wife more than on the husband, and make her change more rapidly into that which she was not. Be she strong or weak, she is apt to revert to her own ways, if she has them, and if she has what is called a will of her own.' And, after a rest and some refreshment Isaac still went on: 'There will not be real union without much self-sacrifice; each chiefly bent on pleasing the other. To most men and women this is not easy; for, what with self-confidence, self-will, self-esteem, and selfishness pure and simple, they enter the marriage state with a foregone conclusion on all the points upon which difference is possible. And there are many. And they will remain stumbling-blocks and rocks of offence, unless one will give way to the other, or both are softened by higher influences.'

'And the wife see that she reverence her husband,' says Paul, with his eye on Rebekah.

Alexander Whyte   *Bible Characters*

Jesus, my strength, my hope,
On thee I cast my care,
With humble confidence look up,
And know thou hear'st my prayer.
Give me on thee to wait,
Till I can all things do,
On thee, almighty to create,
Almighty to renew.

I want a godly fear,
A quick discerning eye
That looks to thee when sin is near,
And sees the tempter fly:
A spirit still prepared,
And armed with jealous care,
For ever standing on its guard
And watching unto prayer.

I want a true regard,
A single, steady aim,
Unmoved by threatening or reward,
To thee and thy great name;
A jealous, just concern
For thine immortal praise;
A pure desire that all may learn
And glorify thy grace.

I rest upon thy word;
The promise is for me;
My succour and salvation, Lord,
Shall surely come from thee:
But let me still abide,
Nor from my hope remove,
Till thou my patient spirit guide
Into thy perfect love.

Charles Wesley 1707-88

God, who made me, you know the flaws in my character. Help me to realize that growing older may not always mean growing sweeter or better. Deal with my selfishness and self-will before they spread unchecked.
Give me grace to submit to others. Teach me to possess that ornament of a meek and quiet spirit which in your sight is of great price. For Jesus' sake.   Amen.

Day four

Therefore, since we are justified by faith, we have peace with God through our Lord Jesus Christ.

Romans 5:1 RSV

In the evening I went very unwillingly to a society in Aldersgate Street, where one was reading Luther's preface to the Epistle to the Romans. About a quarter before nine, while he was describing the change which God works in the heart through faith in Christ, I felt my heart strangely warmed. I felt I did trust in Christ, Christ alone, for salvation; and an assurance was given me that he had taken away my sins, even mine, and saved me from the law of sin and death.

I began to pray with all my might for those who had in a more especial manner despitefully used me and persecuted me. I then testified openly to all there what I now first felt in my heart. But it was not long before the enemy suggested, 'This cannot be faith; for where is thy joy?' Then was I taught that peace and victory over sin are essential to faith in the Captain of our salvation; but that, as to the transports of joy that usually attend the beginning of it, especially in those who have mourned deeply, God sometimes giveth, sometimes withholdeth, them according to the counsels of his own will.

After my return home, I was much buffeted with temptations, but I cried out, and they fled away. They returned again and again. I as often lifted up my eyes, and he 'sent me help from his holy place'. And herein I found the difference between this and my former state chiefly consisted. I was striving, yea, fighting with all my might under the law, as well as under grace. But then I was sometimes, if not often, conquered; now, I was always conqueror.

From the *Journal of John Wesley*

The Conversion of Saul Kane

I did not think, I did not strive,
The deep peace burnt my me alive;
The bolted door had broken in,
I knew that I had done with sin.
I knew that Christ had given me birth
To brother all the souls on earth,
And every bird and every beast
Should share the crumbs broke at the feast.

O Christ who holds the open gate,
O Christ who drives the furrow straight,
O Christ, the plough, O Christ, the laughter
Of holy white birds flying after,
Lo, all my heart's field red and torn,
And thou wilt bring the young green corn,
The young green corn divinely springing,
The young green corn for ever singing;
And when the field is fresh and fair
Thy blessed feet shall glitter there.
And we will walk the weeded field,
And tell the golden harvest's yield,
The corn that makes the holy bread
By which the soul of man is fed,
The holy bread, the food unpriced,
Thy everlasting mercy, Christ.

John Masefield *The Everlasting Mercy*

Be merciful to me, O God, because of your constant love. Because of your great mercy wipe away my sins! Wash away all my evil and make me clean from my sin! I recognize my faults: I am always conscious of my sins. I have sinned against you — only against you — and done what you consider evil.

Remove my sin, and I will be clean; wash me, and I will be whiter than snow. Create a pure heart in me, O God, and put a new and loyal spirit in me.

Give me again the joy that comes from your salvation, and make me willing to obey you. Through Jesus Christ my Lord.   Amen.

Day five

Be humble towards one another, always considering others better than yourselves.

Philippians 2:3 TEV

'Don't ever attempt, my brothers, to combine snobbery with faith in our glorious Lord Jesus Christ!' In chapter two of his epistle, James gives us a thumb-nail sketch of a first century snob, and tells us that a Christian snob is a contradiction in terms. Are we twentieth century Christians still trying to mix these unmixables? Do we run round the well-dressed person with a top job, to the neglect of the old-age pensioner or the shabby member of our local church? Not guilty? Snobbishness can also take more subtle forms. Do we look down on those who are not intellectual — who had no opportunity for 'higher education' — or whose children have not succeeded where ours have? Or are we 'spiritual' snobs — given to evangelical name-dropping and glad to be on intimate terms with those in the inner Christian circle? Most of us have to admit to being guilty in one or other of these ways.

Paul goes to the heart of the matter when he says, 'Don't become snobbish, but take a real interest in ordinary people' (Rom. 12:16 Phillips). We should be prepared to cultivate the ordinary folk in the church, the ones with less colourful personalities, less stimulating conversation, less gift and ability as well as fewer material assets. To be a snob is to be 'a judge of merit by externals'. God, on the contrary, 'looks on the heart', and 'shows no partiality'. Dare we discriminate where God in his mercy loves us all as his children? 'If you pray to a Father who judges men by their actions without the slightest favouritism, then you should spend the time of your stay here on earth with reverent fear' (1 Pet. 1:17 Phillips). We are all brothers and sisters in the same noble family.

My arm aches from strap hanging.
A rough serge sleeve brushes at my elbow
        to find securer hold.
Looking up, I see a day's stubble on his chin,
        greasy hair,
And dirty scratching fingernails move restlessly,
Imposing on me the rough serge movements
        of his arm.
A Hector Powe shoulder and pig skin case push by
With managerial superiority.
The soured sufficiency of every action
Ignites an indignation in me.
Beyond, a scurfy shoulder, and a woman's face,
Fidgeting constantly:
A nagging twitch in an impassive blank,
Framed by a six-months-old inexpert perm.
Why doesn't she hide her ugliness in shame?

The impressions of every sense
Stir a noxious hate.
I pray to see as Christ would see.

The destructive, impervious hatred
Is twisted into unaccustomed sensations.
Unsatisfied restlessness,
The gildings of prosperity,
The worn-out hopes
Are the only irritants

I catch her eye and smile.
She looks startled, and does not know
        how to respond:
Then a fleeting, new-born smile,
And she is gone.

Rosemary Horner   *Making Eden Grow*

Lord, help me to see others as you see them. May I not be impressed
by good clothes, good looks, wit or polished manners.
Help me not to be put off by shabby dress, uncouth habits, by lack of
money or lack of charm.
You look on the heart. Your love and care are over all your
creatures. Help me to look with your eyes and to let your love flow
through me to others whoever they are. For Jesus' sake.   Amen.

Day six

*Take my yoke upon you, and learn from me; for I am gentle and
lowly in heart, and you will find rest for your souls. For my yoke is
easy, and my burden light.*

Matthew 11:29-30 RSV

It is Jesus' invitation to take his yoke upon our shoulders. The Jews
used the phrase *the yoke* for *entering into submission to*. They spoke
of the yoke of the Law, the yoke of the commandments, the yoke of
the Kingdom, the yoke of God. But it may well be that Jesus took the
words of his invitation from something much nearer home than that.
He says, 'My yoke is *easy*.' The word *easy* is in Greek *chrestos*,
which can mean *well-fitting*. In Palestine ox-yokes were made of
wood; the ox was brought, and the measurements were taken. The
yoke was then roughed out, and the ox was brought back to have the
yoke tried on. The yoke was then carefully adjusted, so that it would
fit well, and would not gall the neck of the patient beast. The yoke
was tailor-made to fit the ox. Now there is a legend that Jesus made
the best ox-yokes in all Galilee, and that from all over the country
men came to him to the carpenter's shop to buy the best yokes that
skill could make. In those days, as now, shops had their signs above
the door; and it has been suggested that the sign above the door of
the carpenter's shop in Nazareth may well have been: 'My yokes fit
well.' It may well be that Jesus is here using a picture from the
carpenter's shop in Nazareth where he had worked throughout the
silent years.

So Jesus says, 'My yoke fits well.' What he says is: 'The life I give
you to live is not a burden to gall you; your task, your life, is made to
measure to fit you.' Whatever God sends to us is made to fit our
needs and our abilities exactly; God has a task for every one of us,
which is made to measure for us. Jesus says, 'My burden is light.' As
a Rabbi had it: 'My burden is become my song.' It is not that the
burden is easy to carry; but it is laid on us in love; it is meant to be
carried in love, and love makes even the heaviest burden light.

William Barclay   *The Daily Study Bible*

Forth in thy name, O Lord, I go,
My daily labour to pursue,
Thee, only thee, resolved to know
In all I think, or speak, or do.

The task thy wisdom has assigned
O let me cheerfully fulfil,
In all my works thy presence find,
And prove thy good and perfect will.

Thee may I set at my right hand,
Whose eyes my inmost substance see,
And labour on at thy command,
And offer all my works to thee.

Give me to bear thy easy yoke,
And every moment watch and pray,
And still to things eternal look,
And hasten to thy glorious day:

For thee delightfully employ
Whate'er thy bounteous grace hath given,
And run my course with even joy,
And closely walk with thee to heaven.

Charles Wesley 1707-88

O God, renew our spirits by thy Holy Spirit, and draw our hearts this morning unto thyself, that our work may not be a burden, but a delight; and give us such a mighty love to thee as may sweeten all our obedience. Let us not serve with the spirit of bondage as slaves, but with cheerfulness and gladness, as children, delighting ourselves in thee and rejoicing in thy wishes for the sake of Jesus Christ.

Amen.

Benjamin Jenks 1647-1724

Day seven

My grace is sufficient for you.

2 Corinthians 12:9 RSV

Then I saw in my dream that the Interpreter took Christian by the hand, and led him into a place where was a fire burning against a wall, and one standing by it, always casting much water upon it, to quench it; yet did the fire burn higher and hotter.

Then said Christian, What means this?

The Interpreter answered, This fire is the work of grace that is wrought in the heart; he that casts water upon it, to extinguish and put it out, is the Devil; but in that thou seest the fire notwithstanding burn higher and hotter, thou shalt also see the reason of that. So he had him about to the backside of the wall, where he saw a man with a vessel of oil in his hand, of the which he did also continually cast, but secretly, into the fire.

Then said Christian, What means this?

The Interpreter answered, This is Christ, who continually, with the oil of his grace, maintains the work already begun in the heart: by the means of which, notwithstanding what the devil can do, the souls of his people prove gracious still (2 Cor. 12:9). And in that thou sawest that the man stood behind the wall to maintain the fire, that is to teach thee that it is hard for the tempted to see how this work of grace is maintained in the soul.

John Bunyan   *Pilgrim's Progress*

A sovereign protector I have,
Unseen, yet for ever at hand,
Unchangeably faithful to save,
Almighty to rule and command.
He smiles, and my comforts abound;
His grace as the dew shall descend,
And walls of salvation surround
The soul he delights to defend.

Inspirer and hearer of prayer,
Thou shepherd and guardian of thine,
My all to thy covenant care
I sleeping and waking resign.
If thou art my shield and my sun,
The night is no darkness to me;
And fast as my moments roll on,
They bring me but nearer to thee.

Augustus Toplady 1740-78

May the strength of God pilot us. May the power of God preserve us. May the wisdom of God instruct us. May the hand of God protect us. May the way of God direct us. May the shield of God defend us. May the host of God guard us against the snares of evil and the temptations of the world.
May Christ be with us, Christ before us, Christ in us, Christ over us. May thy salvation, O Lord, be always ours this day and for evermore. Amen.

St Patrick's Breastplate

Day eight

I will praise you, Lord, with all my heart; I will tell of all the wonderful things you have done.

Psalm 9:1 TEV

I never did have much time for Pollyanna, that heroine of girls' books who always found something to be glad about, however uncongenial her circumstances. After all, when life is unpleasant and events go badly wrong a good moan can bring great relief. But perhaps in contrast to Pollyanna, we have become so used to seeing the snags and so addicted to complaining that we have seriously neglected the Scriptural injunction to be thankful.

The fact that we are commanded to be thankful implies that there is something positive for us to do about it. Most run of the mill situations, after all, contain ingredients both for good and ill. The family may bring us problems and even sadness but absence of family can undoubtedly do the same. My Victorian house presents endless difficulties with cleaning and decorating but on the other hand it affords us soundproof walls and room to spread out. In every situation we should try honestly to see the good as well as the bad — then emphasize the good. The way we interpret life can become a habit. We all know people with a flair for being satisfied with their lot and others with a positive talent for feeling hard done by.

A spoilt child is never satisfied with the presents he receives or the choices offered him by his parents. Perhaps as Christians we may have become spoilt, continually discontented with the choice afforded us or the gifts given to us by our heavenly Father. Every new day, with its potential for happiness and sadness, high drama or dull routine, is a gift from God. We can respond by reminding ourselves, 'This is the day which the Lord has made; let us be glad and rejoice in it'. We are not intended to look at life constantly through rose-tinted spectacles. With realistic appraisal of the facts and emphasizing the good in our lot, we can look steadily at each day, knowing that what comes is known to God and can be received and used by us with thankful hearts. As Christians our thankfulness is not empty optimism or wishful thinking but is grounded in solid experience of what God has done for us in the past and what he is continuing to do for us through Christ. So 'Let the peace of Christ rule in your hearts . . . and be thankful' (Col. 3:15 RSV).

King of glory, King of peace
  I will love thee:
And that love may never cease,
  I will move thee.

Thou hast granted my request,
  Thou hast heard me:
Thou didst note my working breast,
  Thou hast spared me.

Wherefore with my utmost art
  I will sing thee,
And the cream of all my heart
  I will bring thee.

Seven whole days, not one in seven,
  I will praise thee.
In my heart, though not in heaven,
  I can raise thee.

Small it is in this poor sort
  To enrol thee,
Ev'n eternity is too short
  To extol thee.

George Herbert 1593-1633

Lord, make my life full of thankfulness and praise. Every day brings me your love, your care, and your presence with me. Thank you, Lord, for everything. Amen.

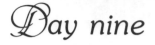
Day nine

When word reached the king of Judah . . . he and all his people were so terrified that they trembled like leaves shaking in the wind. The Lord said to Isaiah, 'Tell him to keep alert, to stay calm, and not to be frightened or disturbed'.

Isaiah 7:2-4 TEV

King Ahaz of Judah was in a tizzy — and small wonder. In one direction lay the great and brutal power of Assyria and in the other the machinations of Egypt. Nearer, much nearer, were Syria and Israel, ready to march on Jerusalem, topple Ahaz from his throne, and force Judah into their hopeless alliance against Assyria. Deep fear and a desperate sense of weakness assailed this poor specimen of kingship. In a panic of activity he rushed to inspect the city's water supply in readiness for the expected siege. God's prophet, Isaiah, came to meet him with words from the Lord: Don't be frightened of your approaching enemies — they are no more dangerous than 'two smouldering sticks'. What a way to dismiss two such menacing opponents! They were nothing more in God's reckoning than a couple of damp squibs, about to fizzle out without so much as a bang. Future events may seem ominous and real to us as they loom threateningly close. 'Stay calm, do not be frightened,' God says to us, knowing how unfounded our fears so often are.

Isaiah goes on to exhort the vacillating king to build up his crumbling faith rather than his defences. So often we dash here and there making plans and taking action as a cover up for our inward uncertainty and weakness. Calmness of mind and firm faith in God are better antidotes to fear than frantic planning and hectic activity. To those who wait with trust for him to act on their behalf, God still promises the strength to stand firm whatever comes. The enemy at the door will not engulf us.

We rest on thee, our Shield and our Defender!
We go not forth alone against the foe;
Strong in thy strength, safe in thy keeping tender,
We rest on thee and in thy name we go.

Yes, in thy name, O Captain of salvation!
In thy dear name, all other names above;
Jesus our righteousness, our sure Foundation,
Our Prince of glory and our King of love.

We go in faith, our own great weakness feeling,
And needing more each day thy grace to know:
Yet from our hearts a song of triumph pealing;
We rest on thee and in thy name we go.

Edith Gilling Cherry (d. 1897)

Lord, quieten my heart and mind. Help me to be still and know that you are God in the whole earth. Then help me to get on with the task ahead calmly and in your strength alone.   Amen.

$\mathcal{D}$ay ten

Behold, I stand at the door and knock; if any one hears my voice and opens the door, I will come in to him and eat with him, and he with me.

Revelation 3:20 RSV

I pass over a ridge in the road on the journey from the city to my home on the western hills. If it is broad day, I see from the road's bend the tiles of home against the forest green; at night I know that one of the distant lights, where they climb and scatter against the western darkness, is all my own. 'Home', said the Roman proverb, 'is where the heart is,' and how true are the words. I sit back, and the last four miles slip by. There in yonder patch, is understanding, loyalty and fellowship. Chairs know my shape, and there is rest, the throwing off of armour, the dropping of the guard.

I can imagine no more awful fate than the loss of such priceless things. 'He that has no rest at home', runs a Turkish saying, 'is in the world's hell.'

Look at John 1:11. It runs in the old version: 'He came unto his own, and his own received him not.' The Greek text runs, literally translated, 'He came to his own things, and his own people did not receive him.' In John 19:27 the Greek runs again, quite literally, 'From that hour that disciple took Mary to *his own things*.' Could it be more clear that in the common dialect of Greek in which the New Testament is written, the phrase 'one's own things' meant home? So translate John 1:11: 'He came home and his own people turned him from the door.'

All the pathos of Christ's rejection is in the sentence. Through the long centuries of her history God had been building a home in Palestine. Its walls were the devotion and faith of a uniquely enlightened people, trained by the law and the prophets to recognize 'the day of their visitation'. It was in their power to know the purpose of God, but they misunderstood and distorted it. And so they spoilt God's building, and when, in Christ, he came to the door in the land and universe of his own creation, his own folk did not know him, and turned him away.

E M Blaiklock

Come in, O come! the door stands open now;
I knew thy voice: Lord Jesus, it was thou;
The sun has set long since; the storms begin;
'Tis time for thee, my Saviour, O come in!

Alas, ill-ordered shows the dreary room;
The household stuff lies heaped amidst the gloom;
The table empty stands, the couch undressed;
Ah, what a welcome for the Eternal Guest!

Yet welcome, and today; this doleful scene
Is e'en itself my cause to hail thee in;
This dark confusion e'en at once demands
Thine own bright presence, Lord, and
    ordering hands.

I seek no more to alter thing, or mend,
Before the coming of so great a Friend;
All were at best unseemly and 'twere ill
Beyond all else to keep thee waiting still.

Come, not to find, but make this troubled heart
A dwelling worthy of thee as thou art;
To chase the gloom, the terror, and the sin:
Come, all thyself, yea come, Lord Jesus, in!

Handley Moule 1841-1920

Lord Jesus, forgive me that I too have many times turned you away from your rightful dwelling place. Make your home within me now and rule there as Master and Lord.   Amen.

$\mathcal{D}$ay eleven

God opposes the proud, but gives grace to the humble.
James 4:6 RSV

Before finishing, I want to guard against two misunderstandings. First of all, don't think Pride is something God forbids because he is offended at it, or that Humility is something he demands as due to his own dignity — as if God himself was proud. He is not in the least worried about his dignity. The point is, he wants you to know him: wants to give you himself. And he and you are two things of such a kind that if you really get into any kind of touch with him you will, in fact, be humble — delightedly humble, feeling the infinite relief of having for once got rid of all the silly nonsense about *your* dignity which has made you restless and unhappy all your life. He is trying to make you humble in order to make this moment possible: trying to take off a lot of silly, ugly, fancy-dress in which we have all got ourselves up and are strutting about like the little idiots we are. I wish I had got a bit further with humility myself: if I had, I could probably tell you more about the relief, the comfort, of taking the fancy-dress off — getting rid of the false self, with all its 'Look at me' and 'Aren't I a good boy?' and all its posing and posturing. To get even near it, even for a moment, is like a drink of cold water to a man in a desert.

The second point is this. Don't imagine that if you meet a really humble man he will be what most people call 'humble' nowadays: he won't be a sort of greasy, smarmy person, who's always telling you that, of course, he's nobody. Probably all you'll think about him is that he seemed a cheerful, intelligent chap who took a real interest in what *you* said to *him*. If you *do* dislike him it will be because you feel a little envious of anyone who seems to enjoy life so easily. He won't be thinking about humility: he won't be thinking about himself at all. There I must stop. If anyone would like to acquire humility, I can, I think, tell him the first step. The first step is to realise that one is proud. And a biggish step, too. At least, nothing whatever can be done before it. If you think you're not conceited, it means you are very conceited indeed.

C S Lewis   Christian Behaviour

He that is down needs fear no fall;
He that is low, no pride;
He that is humble, ever shall
Have God to be his guide.
I am content with what I have,
Little be it, or much;
And, Lord, contentment still I crave,
Because thou savest such.
Fulness to such, a burden is,
That go on pilgrimage;
Here little, and hereafter bliss,
Is best from age to age.

John Bunyan   The Shepherd Boy's Song
— *Pilgrim's Progress*

Lord, you wanted it, here I am on the ground.
I don't even dare rise, I don't even dare look at you.
Nothing, I am nothing, I know it now.
Your light is terrible, Lord, and I'd like to escape it.
Since I have accepted you, you have bared my dwelling,
Every day, mercilessly, your light uncovers it,
And I see what I had never seen before.

Formerly, I admitted that I was a sinner, that I was unworthy,
And I believed it, Lord, but I didn't know it.
In your presence I looked for some faults
But produced only laboured and feeble confessions.
Lord, it's my whole being that kneels now,
It's the sin that I am that asks forgiveness.

Lord, thank you for your light — I would never have known.
But, Lord, enough. I assure you I've understood.
I am *nothing*
And you are *all.*

Michel Quoist   *Prayers of Life*

$\mathcal{D}$ay twelve

No kind of hurt was found upon him, because he had trusted in his God.

Daniel 6:23 RSV

What a surprising conclusion the writer of this famous story draws! We might have ended by saying 'No kind of hurt was found upon him because God's power was greater than the lions'. And we should have been right. But for the writer such a comment was too obvious to need underlining. What does not go without saying is that Daniel had a part to play in the deliverance God gave. Of course God can act in glorious isolation but in his wonderful grace he chooses most often to act in partnership with human beings. In salvation and in all the experiences of Christian living, Scripture teaches that God chooses to harness his power to our faith. He is free to act to the extent that we trust him.

The converse is true. In his home town Jesus 'did not do many mighty works . . . because of their unbelief'. God's omnipotence can actually be limited by our lack of answering faith.

The reason surely lies in God's deep desire to form relationships with us. He is no detached miracle worker but a personal God who wants us to share an experience with him, not merely admire an all-powerful Being at work. In this way we come to know him better. God could have provided an escape clause so that Darius reprieved Daniel from his night among the lions. God chose instead to let Daniel go through the experience and in so doing come to know God better. Darius and many others came to believe in God too. God will choose how best to deal with our particular den of lions. His aim is to further our knowledge of him. We may be rescued from or through our difficulties. That is God's affair. It is for us to trust him. When we trust God we can be sure that he will act in power for his glory and our good.

Give me the faith which can remove
And sink the mountain to a plain;
Give me the child-like praying love
Which longs to build your house again;
Your love, let it my heart o'erpower,
And fill me from this very hour.

My talents, gifts, and graces, Lord,
Into your blessed hands receive,
And let me live to preach your word,
And let me to your glory live;
My every sacred moment spend
In publishing the sinner's Friend.

Charles Wesley 1707-88

I hand over to your care, Lord,
My soul and body
My mind and thoughts
My prayers and my hopes
My health and my work
My life and my death
My parents and my family
My friends and my neighbours
My country and all men
Today
And always.

Lancelot Andrewes 1555-1626

B

$\mathcal{D}$ay thirteen

Stand firm and steady. Keep busy always in your work for the Lord, since you know that nothing you do in the Lord's service is ever useless.

1 Corinthians 15:58 TEV

> Don't grieve for me now
> Don't grieve for me never,
> I'm going to do nothing
> For ever and ever.

So runs the legendary epitaph for a charlady. With a little more decorum and grammar we sometimes sing:

> So now to watch! to work! to war!
> And then to rest for ever!

I don't suppose any of us really cherishes a picture of Heaven as a place of endless inactivity but the thought of no more work certainly has its attraction. The trouble with work, like so many other things in life, is that it rarely comes in well regulated quantities. Most of us have had an occasional experience of lying immobile in a hospital ward. At such times we contemplate the thought of a stack of washing up as a positive pleasure. Most of the time we are faced with a stack of washing up and long for the chance to have a quiet sit down.

It is only as we get away from *our* definition of work and begin to think in terms of *God's* definition that some of these extremes are reconciled. Work, from God's viewpoint, is the fulfilling of whatever he, in his infinite wisdom, has planned. Every one of us, as his children, has a unique work to do towards the bringing in of his kingdom. 'She can only pray', we may sadly conclude of a Christian who is elderly or disabled. In so saying we fail to recognize that such a person is probably privileged to carry out the highest and hardest work that God assigns his children.

Because we are human, most of us will continue to experience from time to time the frustrations that beset our particular situation. Yet, deep down, we acknowledge that to recognize the work that God is giving us and to accept it from his hand is the key to peace and contentment. Our work is of *his* choosing. Jesus Christ said, 'My food is to obey the will of the one who sent me and to finish the work he gave me to do' (John 4:34 TEV). May God give us grace to follow in the Master's steps.

34

Jesus, Master, whose I am,
Purchased thine alone to be,
By thy blood, O spotless Lamb,
Shed so willingly for me,
Let my heart be all thine own,
Let me live to thee alone.

Jesus, Master, whom I serve,
Though so feebly and so ill,
Strengthen hand and heart and nerve
All thy bidding to fulfil;
Open thou mine eyes to see
All the work thou hast for me.

Jesus, Master, wilt thou use
One who owes thee more than all?
As thou wilt! I would not choose;
Only let me hear thy call.
Jesus, let me always be,
In thy service, glad and free

Frances Ridley Havergal 1836-79

Lord, establish thou the work of our hands upon us, yea, the work of our hands establish thou it.   Amen.

Day fourteen

Even the Son of Man did not come to be served; he came to serve and to give his life to redeem many people.

Mark 10:45 TEV

'When I was quite young I used to go down to the slums of London. I would go into a common lodging house on a Sunday night dressed in a frock coat and a silk top hat and I would stand there with a Testament in my hand and preach and preach, and be very much surprised that the people did not listen to me. I was enormously impressed at their iniquity! Here was a young man in a frock coat and a silk top hat, and they didn't even listen to him! Then I discovered the reason *why* they didn't listen, and I got hold of the oldest suit I could borrow and in the pocket of that suit I placed the sum of 4d., and in the evening I went, with the rag-tag and bobtail of the district, to that lodging house where two or three hundred men were to sleep for the night. I sat where they sat, and the fleas that bit them bit me; and the same crawly things that crawled on them crawled on me. I spent some nights in that dreadful chamber silently listening to their needs and woes. Then at six o'clock one morning when they were getting their breakfast, I arose and began to speak to them, and now I found there was not the slightest difficulty in obtaining their attention. I had sat where they sat, generally for about nine wakeful hours, and I understood exactly how dirty they were, how the seas of life were buffeting them, and they were perfectly willing to listen to a man who had sat where they sat. And the greatest day in our history was the day when it came to the heart of God to draw closer to us than he had ever done before. After forty centuries of dwelling in cloud and thick darkness, it came to the heart of God to come closer to us. But he did not send his Son to start preaching some code: when our Lord went into the business of Redemption, for thirty years he never said a word of public ministry. For thirty years he sat where men sat and learned their thoughts and experiences. For thirty years he knew hunger, weariness, poverty, and the shadows and cares of that little home, and when he had learned all these things, then he opened his mouth and began to speak. And the world has been listening ever since.'

Patricia St John   Harold St John
— A Portrait by his Daughter

O Master, let me walk with thee
In lowly paths of service free;
Tell me thy secret; help me bear
The strain of toil, the fret of care.

Help me the slow of heart to move
By some clear, winning word of love;
Teach me the wayward feet to stay,
And guide them in the homeward way.

Teach me thy patience; still with thee
In closer, dearer company,
In work that keeps faith sweet and strong,
In trust that triumphs over wrong;

In hope that sends a shining ray
Far down the future's broadening way;
In peace that only thou canst give,
With thee, O Master, let me live.

Washington Gladden 1836-1918

Father, make me sacrificial in my service to others.
I want to be willing to say no to self and to spend on others the kind
of loving care and understanding that I so often lavish on myself.
Give me the imagination to understand how others are feeling and
the generosity to share their troubles and if need be their hardships,
so that I may show them the love of Christ by my actions as well as
my words. For Jesus' sake.   Amen.

Day fifteen

A cloud overshadowed them, and a voice came out of the cloud,
'This is my beloved Son; listen to him.' And suddenly looking around
they no longer saw any one with them but Jesus only.

Mark 9:7-8 RSV

1. 'Speak, Lord, because your servant hears. I am your servant.
Give me understanding that I may know your testimonies. Incline my
heart to the words of your mouth. Let your speech flow as the dew.'
Once the children of Israel would say to Moses: 'Do you speak to us,
and we will hear. Let not the Lord speak to us lest perchance we die.'
Not so, Lord, not so, do I pray, but rather, with Samuel the Prophet,
humbly and longingly I make supplication: 'Speak, Lord, because
your servant hears.' Let not Moses speak to me, or any of the
Prophets, but do you rather speak, Lord God, who inspired and
enlightened all the Prophets; because you alone, without them, can
perfectly instruct me, but they, without you, will profit nothing.

2. They can, indeed, sound words, but cannot convey the spirit.
They speak most beautifully, but, with you silent, they do not fire the
heart. They hand scriptures on to us, but you open up the meaning
of the signs. They issue commands, but you help to perform them.
They show the way, but you give strength to walk in it. They function
only outside of us, but you instruct and enlighten the heart. They
water the surface, but you give fertility. They cry aloud with words,
but you give understanding to the hearer.

3. Let not Moses, therefore, speak to me, but you, O Lord, my
God, Eternal Truth, lest I die and prove fruitless, if I shall have been
admonished without, but not fired within; and lest the word heard,
but not done, known, but not loved, believed, and not kept, serve
for judgment against me. 'Speak, therefore, Lord, because your
servant hears; for you have the words of eternal life.' Speak to me,
for some sort of comfort to my soul, and for the mending of my
whole life, but to your praise and glory and everlasting honour.

Thomas à Kempis *The Imitation of Christ*
(translated by E M Blaiklock)

Speak, Lord, in the stillness,
While I wait on thee;
Hushed my heart to listen
In expectancy.

Speak, O blessed Master,
In this quiet hour;
Let me see thy face, Lord,
Feel thy touch of power.

Speak, thy servant heareth!
Be not silent, Lord:
Waits my soul upon thee
For the quickening word!

Fill me with the knowledge
Of thy glorious will;
All thine own good pleasure
In thy child fulfil.

E May Grimes 1868-1927

Lord, today, teach me to listen.
'There is a time for silence and a time for speech', so say the Scriptures. Lord, teach me the silence of humility, the silence of wisdom, the silence of love, the silence of perfection, the silence that speaks without words, the silence of faith.
Saviour, teach me to silence my heart that I may listen to the gentle movement of the Holy Spirit within me and sense the depths which are God today and always.

Sixteenth century   Frankfurt

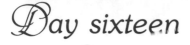

Day sixteen

The Lord is merciful and gracious, slow to anger and abounding in steadfast love. He will not always chide, nor will he keep his anger for ever.

As a father pities his children, so the Lord pities those who fear him.

Psalm 103: 8, 9, 13 RSV

He has a sovereign right to do with us as he pleases; and if we consider what we are, surely we shall confess we have no reason to complain: and to those who seek him, his sovereignty is exercised in a way of grace. All shall work together for good: everything is needful that he sends; nothing can be needful that he withholds. Be content to bear the cross; others have borne it before you. You have need of patience; and if you ask, the Lord will give it: but there can be no settled peace till our will is in a measure subdued. Hide yourself under the shadow of his wings; rely upon his care and power; look upon him as a physician who has graciously undertaken to heal your soul of the worst of sicknesses, sin. Yield to his prescriptions, and fight against every thought that would represent it as desirable to be permitted to choose for yourself. When you cannot see your way, be satisfied that he is your leader. When your spirit is overwhelmed within you, he knows your path: he will not leave you to sink. He has appointed seasons of refreshment, and you shall find he does not forget you. Above all, keep close to the throne of grace. If we seem to get no good by attempting to draw near him, we may be sure we shall get none by keeping away from him.

John Newton Select Letters

Begone unbelief!
My Saviour is near,
And for my relief
Will surely appear.
By prayer let me wrestle,
And he will perform:
With Christ in the vessel,
I smile at the storm.

If dark be my way,
Since he is my guide,
'Tis mine to obey,
'Tis his to provide:
Though cisterns be broken,
And creatures all fail,
The word he hath spoken
Shall surely prevail.

His love in time past
Forbids me to think
He'll leave me at last
In trouble to sink:
Each sweet Ebenezer
I have in review
Confirms his good pleasure
To help me quite through.

Since all that I meet
Shall work for my good,
The bitter is sweet,
The medicine is food;
Though painful at present,
'Twill cease before long;
And then, O how pleasant
The conqueror's song!

John Newton 1725-1807

Lord Jesus Christ, you were poor
and in distress, a captive and forsaken as I am.
You know all man's troubles;
You abide with me when all men fail me;
You remember and seek me;
It is your will that I should know you and turn to you.
Lord, I hear your call and follow;
Help me . . .

Lord, whatever this day may bring,
Your name be praised.
O God, be gracious to me and help me.
Give me strength to bear what you send,
and do not let fear rule over me;
I trust in your grace
and commit my life wholly into your hands.

Do with me according to your will
and as is best for me.
Whether I live or die, I am with you,
and you, my God, are with me.
Lord, I wait for your salvation
and for your kingdom.

Dietrich Bonhoeffer from 'Prayer for His Fellow Prisoners,
Christmas 1943'

Day seventeen

Examine yourselves: are you living the life of faith?
                                                    2 Corinthians 13:5 NEB

It is only too easy to criticize the way other Christians are living. The Corinthian Christians were criticizing the apostle Paul himself. In his second letter Paul vindicates himself and then turns the tables on his accusers: 'Examine yourselves — are *you* living the life of faith?'

The first characteristic of such a life of faith is that it rests on God's promises and God's rewards. All day and every day we make choices and decisions, and they are influenced by our aims in life. Whether it's the neighbourhood we choose to live in, the church we choose to join, or the people we invite to tea, we are working with a definite purpose in mind. When Moses chose his life-style, we are told that he 'looked steadily to the ultimate, not the immediate reward'. Because he was living the life of faith he reckoned on God's reward and was prepared to forego all the advantages of Pharaoh's court.

We also live the life of faith by resting in God's strength as well as in his promises. Perhaps we feel inadequate to cope with our organized routine, yet we struggle on, too proud to admit the failures or to admit our need. But an honest recognition of weakness is the first step in the life of faith. 'When I am weak, then I am strong,' Paul asserted. When I come to the end of my own efforts I am ready by faith to appropriate Christ for all my needs — 'then the power of Christ will come and rest upon me.'

How much, as normal sinful human beings, we shrink from living by faith and long to live by sight. We want rewards that we can see and touch. We long for help that is tangible and human. The Christian life is hard because it involves a constant and habitual reckoning on One who cannot yet be seen. 'We walk by faith and not by sight.' Are *we* living the life of faith? Let us examine ourselves.

The Passionate Man's Pilgrimage

Give me my scallop shell of quiet,
My staff of faith to walk upon,
My scrip of joy, immortal diet,
My bottle of salvation:
My gown of glory, hope's true gage,
And thus I'll take my pilgrimage.

Blood must be my body's balmer,
No other balm will there be given,
Whilst my soul, like a white palmer
Travels to the land of heaven,
Over the silver mountains,
Where spring the nectar fountains:
And there I'll kiss
The bowl of bliss,
And drink my eternal fill
On every milken hill.
My soul will be a-dry before,
But after it, will ne'er thirst more.

Sir Walter Raleigh 1552?-1618

Help me today to realize that you will be speaking to me through the events of the day, through people, through things, and through all creation.
Give me ears, eyes and heart to perceive you, however veiled your presence may be.
Give me insight to see through the exterior of things to the interior truth.
Give me your Spirit of discernment!
O Lord, thou knowest how busy I must be this day.
If I forget thee, do not forget me!

Jacob Astley 1579-1652

Day eighteen

Blessed are the poor in spirit; for theirs is the kingdom of heaven.
Matthew 5:3

The liberation this Beatitude brings stems not from the fact that we are poor in spirit *but from the fact that God expects no more*. Every now and then I have met someone who has believed it right to dwell on his or her unworthiness almost to the exclusion of rejoicing in God's continuing accepting kindness. This can lead to terrible depression and can cripple the spirit rather than set it free. Introspection is like some poisonous drugs. Used under doctor's orders in small doses they stimulate and improve health. Used in large doses they destroy.

This, however, might be thought to have little relevance to the matters of identity, mortality and our mixed up inner dynamics; but it has. I am not saying that an insight into the first Beatitude provides a cure for depression. What I am saying is that it is sound therapy to ponder over its meaning. What my 'real self' is matters little. God accepts me as I am and his opinion is the only one that counts. If I must suspect that people are against me the one person who is constantly *for* me is Almighty God. If my inner dynamics are of the type that makes me want to fight to get attention and makes me over-anxious for affection from those around, then the message of the first Beatitude applies to me also. It says, even at my worst, I am accepted by God and favoured by him. It goes further. It says that God's favour is far more than some passing, kindly feeling. It says that I am actually fitted into God's plans — part of his team; for this is the meaning of the words: 'for theirs is the kingdom of heaven'. I *belong*.

Gavin Reid   *A New Happiness*

Thank you God for loving all creation equally,
and for loving me as part of it.
I thank you particularly for putting beyond all question
the fact that it is your nature, character and disposition
*   to love.*
Thank you, therefore, that your love for me does not
depend upon my deserving or my worthiness.
It is such a relief to know that you love me,
not because I am loveable, but because you are love.
I thank you for helping me to see
that my value consists in these two facts:
that you made me, that you love me.
I know now that just as I did not have to do
*   anything in order to be created.*
Neither must I do anything in order to be loved.
I accept completely the fact that you love me
*   unchangeably and forever:*
I accept this as one of the given, unalterable things of life
like the sun which shines whether we deserve it or not.
'God is love.'

Dick Williams   *God Thoughts*

Just as I am, without one plea
But that thy blood was shed for me,
And that thou bidst me come to thee,
O Lamb of God, I come.

Just as I am, thou wilt receive,
Wilt welcome, pardon, cleanse, relieve,
Because thy promise I believe,
O Lamb of God, I come.

Charlotte Elliott 1789-1871

Day nineteen

If anyone wants to follow in my footsteps, he must give up all right to himself, take up his cross and follow me. The man who tries to save his life will lose it; it is the man who loses his life for my sake and the gospel's who will save it.

Mark 8:34-35 Phillips

Every normal woman is equipped to be a mother. Certainly not every woman in the world is destined to make use of the physical equipment but surely motherhood, in a deeper sense, is the essence of womanhood. The body of every normal woman prepares itself repeatedly to receive and to bear. Motherhood requires self-giving, sacrifice, suffering. It is a going down into death in order to give life, a great human analogy of a great spiritual principle (Paul wrote, 'Death worketh in us but life in you'). Womanhood is a call. It is a vocation to which we respond under God, glad if it means the literal bearing of children, thankful as well for all that it means in a much wider sense, that in which every woman, married or single, fruitful or barren, may participate — the unconditional response exemplified for all time in Mary the virgin, and the willingness to enter into suffering, to receive, to carry, to give life, to nurture and to care for others. The strength to answer this call is given us as we look up toward the Love that created us, remembering that it was that Love that first, most literally, *imagined* sexuality, that made us at the very beginning real men and real women. As we conform to that Love's demands we shall become more humble, more dependent — on him and on one another — and even (dare I say it?) more splendid.

Elisabeth Elliot   *Let Me Be A Woman*

All the Children

Lord, I find myself unable to forget the children —
    the children who live in cement shelters,
    the children who eat other people's rubbish,
        who die of neglect and hunger and
            minor illnesses,
    the children who do not know family stability,
    the children who are born to be our hope,
    who deserve food and shelter and clothing and love
        simply because they are living, human beings.
These children are my children
    wherever they are, whoever they are,
    whatever their parents have done or not done
All children are part of my family because
    all children belong to you.
Lord, lead me
    to help meet the needs of children
        everywhere.
Children cannot control their world:
    they are dependent on those of us
        who care for them.
Children need us to nurture them
    so that someday they will be strong enough
        to sustain this ever-changing world.
Help me
    to love my family,
    to provide adequately for them,
    but also to remember my responsibility
        to the human family.

        Judith Mattison   *Prayers from a Mother's Heart*

Lord, you have made me a woman, with a woman's instincts for self-giving and sacrificial love.
Forgive me that instead of giving I spend so much time getting. I am so often selfish and self-indulgent, wanting others to give to me.
Teach me instead to love, comfort and care for others, without counting the cost.
Thank you for the women who 'mothered' you, our Saviour, when you were a baby, a boy and a man on earth. For your sake help me to mother the weak, the comfortless, and the lonely today.   Amen.

Day twenty

I hope . . . to send Timothy . . . I have no one like him, who will be genuinely anxious for your welfare. They all look after their own interests, not those of Jesus Christ.

Philippians 2:19-21 RSV

Have you ever looked forward to meeting a friend so that you could talk about your concerns to a sympathetic listener? Ten minutes later, you discover that *you* have been cast instead in the role of listener. You couldn't get a word in edgeways! And though one person succeeded in doing all the talking, both were in fact wrapped up in their own affairs.

Self-concern is not just a twentieth-century characteristic. The apostle Paul, held fast in prison, yet yearning to go to Philippi to strengthen the Christians there, cast round in his mind to think of some other Christian about him who would share his concern for others. None had the necessary quality — that willingness to lay aside his own concerns and give himself to the needs of others. None except Timothy. In Timothy Paul found a kindred spirit — one other Christian who had the capacity to be concerned for others.

The quality Paul searched for was no rare and unattainable gift, but an attitude of heart that we could all foster, whatever our age or ability. We can begin by being willing, with God's help, to *listen* to other people, when they phone up or stop us in the street, or call at some busy moment. When we really listen we shall become involved enough to care. Care, in turn, leads to prayer and practical action.

If Paul were living today he would still find a desperate shortage of people like Timothy. Perhaps God is looking for us to fill the gap. For, as Paul reminds us, in looking after the interests of others, we are looking after the interests of Jesus Christ.

Question

There was something I wanted to say to you,
But I've forgotten.
Anyway it's been a lovely evening.
It was good just to sit and watch the fire,
To chat and ruffle our feet in the sheepskin rug.
And the coffee and buns, that was nice,
Too.

Yes, that's what I say.
It's so nice not to have to
Think
About anything.

I'll show you to the door.
Now mind the steps,
I'm afraid it's very dark out there.

I remember now
What I wanted to say.
A question it was,
I meant to ask her why she came.

Mig Holder   *Making Eden Grow*

O God, give me grace for this day.
Not for a lifetime, nor for next week, nor for tomorrow, just for
this day.
Direct my thoughts and bless them.
Direct my work and bless it.
Direct the things I say, and give them blessing too.
Direct and bless everything that I think and speak and do.
So that for this one day, just this one day, let me live generously,
kindly, in a state of grace and goodness that denies my many
imperfections and makes me more like you.

Marjorie Holmes   *Lord, Let Me Love*

Day twenty-one

If any one says to you, 'Why are you doing this?' say, 'The Lord has need of it.'

Mark 11:3 RSV

A casual reading of the Gospels might persuade us that a disciple was one who totally abandoned both his possessions and his whole way of life in order to follow Christ. 'We have left everything,' Peter could fairly state. But as we look more closely at the gospel narrative we catch glimpses of many other disciples who continued in their secular calling, maintained their previous life-style yet were ready, within that setting, to give whatever was theirs for the Master's use.

The last week of the Saviour's life was particularly marked — and brightened — by the loving gifts of such disciples, who are often unnamed and otherwise little known. One man lent his colt, another his prepared upper room, yet another his Gethsemane garden. A woman gave her priceless perfume and a man of position used his status as well as his wealth to ensure a worthy burial for his Master.

Many of us are very conscious of being bound by the present pattern of our lives. We cannot break free from circumstances in order to give our whole time to specifically Christian service. There are the legitimate demands of family and secular work. But it is possible for us to use these lawful ties and duties as an excuse for withholding from Christ what we *do* have to give. He does not ask for what we are unable to give but for the offerings that can flow from our particular way of life. Time, talents, experience and advantages in life vary from one to another but all of us have something that the Lord can take and use but which we, out of carelessness, ignorance or selfishness may be withholding.

It may be that we shall be directed by the Holy Spirit to consider channels of giving and service hitherto unknown to us. May we, like David, not be content to give to the Lord that which costs us nothing, but respond in generous self-giving to his need.

The Lord is King! I own his power,
His right to rule each day and hour;
I own his claim on heart and will,
And his demands I would fulfil.

He claims my heart, to keep it clean
From all defiling taint of sin;
He claims my will, that I may prove
How swift obedience answers love.

He claims my hands for active life
In noble deeds and worthy strife;
He claims my feet, that in his ways
I may walk boldly all my days.

He claims my lips that purest word
In all my converse may be heard;
My motives, passions, thoughts, that these
My inner life, my King may please.

O Lord my King, I turn to thee;
Thy loyal service makes me free;
My daily task thou shalt assign;
For heart and will and life are thine.

Darley Terry 1848-1934

Lord God, whose we are and whom we serve,
help us to glorify you this day
    in all the thoughts of our hearts,
    in all the words of our lips,
    and in all the work of our hands,
as become those who are your servants,
through Jesus Christ our Lord.   Amen.

Day twenty-two

Jesus said to them, 'Truly, truly, I say to you, unless you eat the flesh of the Son of man and drink his blood, you have no life in you; he who eats my flesh and drinks my blood has eternal life.

. John 6:53–54 RSV

Not only must we eat and so receive the 'flesh', the full humanity, of him in whom humanity is perfected — the Son of Man; but we must *drink his blood*. The phrase would have been quite as startling, even horrifying, to the Jews as to ourselves. The blood of animals might not be received as food: 'Be sure thou shalt not eat the blood; for the blood is the life; and thou shalt not eat the life with the flesh' (Deut. 12:23; cf. Lev. 17:14, 15, and many similar passages). But the reason why the Jews were forbidden to eat the blood of their sacrifices is itself the reason why we must drink the blood of the Son of Man. The blood is the life; especially is it the life released by death that it may be offered to God.

It is clear that the 'Flesh' and the 'Blood' are thought of as separated and separately received. But flesh from which the blood is separated is dead. We receive the Broken Body; we make our own the 'dying of Jesus' (2 Cor. 4:10). Blood, on the other hand, when poured out, is the life released by death and given to God. As we make our own the 'dying of Jesus', so we make our own the risen life of Jesus, so that in him we may be 'dead unto sin but alive unto God' (Rom. 6:11).

To 'eat the flesh' and to 'drink the blood' of the Son of Man are not the same. The former is to receive the power of self-giving and self-sacrifice to the uttermost. The latter is to receive, in and through that self-giving and self-sacrifice, the life that is triumphant over death and united to God. Both 'elements' are needed for the full act of 'communion' — which suggests that to receive the Holy Communion in one kind only is greviously detrimental to the full reality of the sacrament. The life that gives itself even to death; the life that rises from death into union with God: these are the divine gifts without which *ye have not Life in yourselves*. But he who receives and makes his own those gifts *hath eternal Life*. For those gifts are true food and drink of men; he who receives them and makes them his own *abideth in me and I in him*.

William Temple   *Readings from St John's Gospel*

52

Jesus, thou joy of loving hearts,
Thou Fount of life, thou Light of men,
From the best bliss that earth imparts,
We turn unfilled to thee again.

Thy truth unchanged hath ever stood;
Thou savest those that on thee call;
To them that seek thee thou art good;
To them that find thee, all in all.

We taste thee, O thou living Bread,
And long to feast upon thee still;
We drink of thee, the Fountainhead,
And thirst our souls from thee to fill.

Our restless spirits yearn for thee,
Where'er our changeful lot is cast:
Glad, when thy gracious smile we see;
Blest, when our faith can hold thee fast.

O Jesus, ever with us stay;
Make all our moments calm and bright;
Chase the dark night of sin away;
Shed o'er the world thy holy light.

Latin c. 11th Century,
tr. Ray Palmer 1808-87

Thanks be to thee, our Lord Jesus Christ,
For all the benefits thou hast won for us,
For all the pains and insults thou hast borne for us.
O most merciful Redeemer, Friend and Brother,
May we know thee more clearly,
Love thee more dearly,
And follow thee more nearly; for ever and ever.   Amen.

Richard of Chichester

Day twenty-three

Peter answered, 'I will never leave you, even though all the rest do!'
Mark 14:29 TEV

Then all the disciples left him and ran away.
Mark 14:50 TEV

'I'd love to come but I've promised to . . .' What a useful excuse this can be to wriggle out of an unwanted invitation! But sometimes the invitation is one that we would give our eye teeth to accept — yet insistent in mind and conscience is the knowledge that we have already given our word to do something else far less congenial and attractive on that very day. If only the invitations had come in the reverse order! But a striking mark of the man or woman who is God's friend and companion, says the psalmist, is that he or she is one 'who swears to his own hurt and changes not' (Ps. 15:4). 'He always does what he promises, no matter how much it may cost him' is the TEV translation.

We began with a trivial example — an invitation to a day out, maybe, which clashes with a previous promise to visit an elderly friend or help with a Sunday School tea. Yet it is in the small things that we develop the habits and reactions that assert themselves in the big tests of life. If our life is geared to getting the best for ourselves we shall rearrange the programme no doubt justifying our action salving our conscience suitably. But if we aim to behave as children of our Father in heaven, we shall resolve to reflect the character of the One whose promises are all 'Yes' in Christ.

The most solemn promise we make to another person is in marriage. After a short or longer time some find that in so doing they have sworn to their own hurt. The Christian in such a situation knows the cost of standing by his pledge at the deepest and bitterest level. Those of us not so involved find it easy to say what should be done, but rather we should support in love and in humility those who face such a test. Certainly, whether in the large or the small issues of life the one who 'changes not' can depend on the promise of God with which the psalmist concludes, 'He who does these things shall never be moved' (Ps. 15:5).

Peter

The cock crew: he turned and looked at me.
The eyes that knew the oneness of the stars
And compassed the infinity of heaven,
That saw the universal heart-beat break
Upon the sea-shore of the world of man,
Into the thousand, thousand, drops he seeks
To weld again into a unity:
They burned with the white agony of love
Into my soul.
      The cock's cry rent the night.
I knew the unity that I had rent:
I saw the great gulf of my sin and self,
And longed to expiate the thing I was.
While I relied on him for every breath,
For every sense, for every step and hope
I thought to cross the gulf of sin alone.
The third time the cock crew.
      Beyond the fire,
Forged in the flame at which I warmed my hands,
I saw a cross: it was not I who bled.
I could not suffer to redeem myself:
I had denied him: Jesus stood alone.
This was my sin. This was my ransom price.
This was the shattered unity resolved.

I wept myself out of my soul that night,
And through the fire and tears he came to fill me.

           Mary Chandler   *Making Eden Grow*

Thank you, Lord, that you are faithful to your promises.
    You have promised to forgive and cleanse when we confess our sin. Forgive me now for broken promises, forgotten vows and unkept resolves.
Make me more like you — trustworthy, reliable, a woman of my word.
    That I may be a true daughter of my Father in heaven.   Amen.

Day twenty-four

Let God re-mould your minds from within.

Romans 12:2 Phillips

When the Duke of Edinburgh addressed the General Assembly of the Church of Scotland, he suggested that objectors to free comment should wear a label round their necks saying: 'My mind was made up long ago, don't confuse me with any other ideas'. I wonder how many of us qualify for such a label? Some of us may have taken over, ready-made, the opinions of a former generation. Others of us may close our minds to new ideas out of a genuine if mistaken effort to counteract the laxness of present-day standards.

I believe that for many reasons a closed mind is not merely regrettable — it is a threat to spiritual life. In our Lord's day, closed minds blinded religious, good-living people to the Messiah they looked for. In contrast, the members of the early Church were open, flexible. If they had not been, the gospel would never have been preached to us Gentiles and, later on, the requirements of Jewish law would have been imposed on all believers. God cannot make his ways known to a closed mind.

A person who never changes her mind is bound to be immature. We must change if we are to grow in anything more than years. We rightly expect an old Christian to be more tolerant than a young one. Our circumstances, the people we meet, growing experience, should all modify our thinking. Of course we must hold tenaciously to the unchanging tenets of our faith, but where godly men differ we dare not be dogmatic. Young people are taught at school to learn by discussion. If we are to be any help to them spiritually we too must learn to discuss amicably, to see the other's viewpoint and admit, when necessary, that we have been mistaken. Pride and laziness too often hinder us. It takes humility to continue to be a disciple instead of claiming to have all the answers. It takes effort to refuse to sink into the ease of a ready-made view and instead sift the evidence so that we may be workmen 'with nothing to be ashamed of, and who know how to use the word of truth to the best advantage'.

I have been giving thought, Lord
　　— you have a minute? — to getting old.
Natural enough as the years pass.

Getting old, a fellow said, is all in the mind.
True. It's also inclined to get into the joints,
　　the digestion, and the poor old feet.
Spectacles appear, then a second pair.
Certain powers wane. Expected; allowed for.
But the fellow's right, or nearly right.

Now, Lord. To the point.
What if the mind gets stiff in the joints?
　　Where are you then?
What if the mind goes lame, needs two pairs of specs?
Then, it would seem, a person's got trouble.
I mean, if the mind is in charge, and
　　starts taking days off; loses grip.
　　Where are you then?
Seems it's time for a person to shut the office.

So, Lord, please keep me young in the mind.
　　Let me enjoy, Lord, let me enjoy.
If creaky I must be, and many-spectacled,
　　and morning-stiff and food-careful,
If trembly-handed and slow-moving and
　　breath-short and head-noddy,
I won't complain. Not a word
If, with your help, dear Friend, there
　　will dwell in this ancient monument,
A Young Mind. Please, Lord?

　　　　David Kossoff   *You Have a Minute, Lord?*

Lord, give me the grace to change my mind:
　　To revise my hasty judgements of other people instead of
　　　　blacklisting them in my mind for ever after;
　　To moderate or modify my views on doubtful matters, where
　　　　godly men and women hold opposite opinions,
Keep my mind open to receive fresh ideas from yourself
　　　　through your Word, through your servants
　　　　and through the world about me.   Amen.

Day twenty-five

Jesus also told this parable . . . "Once there were two men who went up to the Temple to pray: one was a Pharisee, the other a tax collector.
The Pharisee stood apart by himself and prayed, 'I thank you, God, that I am not greedy, dishonest, or an adulterer, like everybody else. I thank you that I am not like that tax collector over there. I fast two days a week, and I give you a tenth of all my income.'
But the tax collector stood at a distance and would not even raise his face to heaven, but beat on his breast and said, 'God, have pity on me, a sinner!' I tell you," said Jesus, "the tax collector, and not the Pharisee, was in the right with God when he went home."

Luke 18:9-14 TEV

Do people need to hear the doctrine of this parable today? Certainly they do. It is a complete delusion to think that legalism is dead.

Many people — church people no less than multitudes outside the church who would not call themselves atheists — still try to square their consciences by telling themselves that they have done their duty, and for the rest they put their faith in an easy-osy God like Omar Khayyam's: 'He's a good fellow and 'twill all be well'.

Tell them that the Almighty God is gracious, speak to them of his forgiveness, and they listen without understanding, persuaded that they have no need to repent. Only when they learn how insufficient is all their boasted goodness — only when they become dissatisfied not with this or that fault in their lives but with their whole character, that they are ready to cry with the publican, 'God, be merciful to me a sinner!' or with Thomas Chalmers, 'What could I do if God did not justify the ungodly?' — only then will they realize that the Gospel speaks to their condition and offers them the remedy they need. 'It is the beggars before God who are blessed,' said the Lord. 'Yes,' added Martin Luther, 'and we are all beggars.' But not till we know that we are beggars can we receive God's grace. This is the truth of our parable, and it is timeless.

A M Hunter   *Interpreting the Parables*

None other Lamb, none other name,
None other hope in heaven or earth or sea,
None other hiding-place from guilt and shame,
None beside thee.

My faith burns low, my hope burns low;
Only my heart's desire cries out in me,
By the deep thunder of its want and woe,
Cries out to thee.

Lord, thou art life, though I be dead;
Love's fire thou art, however cold I be;
Nor heaven have I, nor place to lay my head,
Nor home, but thee.

Christina Rossetti (1830-94)

Father, forgive me today for my smugness and self-satisfaction
    Forgive me for thinking that I have done as well as my
        neighbour or rather better.
    Forgive me for going over my little triumphs — good deeds,
        kind actions — and imagining that you are admiring them
            and will put them down to my credit.
    Show me myself as I really am, with all my selfishness and
        self-indulgence, my self-interest and self-concern.

Lord, have mercy on me, forgive me and make me clean
    not because of any good in me
    but through the blood of Jesus Christ your Son
        and for his sake.   Amen.

Day twenty-six

Whoever would be great among you must be your servant, and whoever would be first among you must be slave of all. For the Son of man also came not to be served but to serve, and to give his life as a ransom for many.

Mark 10:43 RSV

The motto of the Prince of Wales — I Serve — sounds a little out of date to modern ears. Young girls no longer 'go into service' and nurses, police, firemen and teachers, who at one time considered it their privilege to serve the community, are today often taken up with their rights and rewards.

Yet much of the Christian life can still be summed up in the word service. Not only are we God's servants, but as the New Testament constantly reminds us, we are to serve and submit to others. Perhaps as women we *do* spend a good bit of our life running round others — our family, our boss, the members of our local church — but we often do it with resentment and grumbles. So many of the jobs may not seem worthy of our time and effort. Our own personalities may seem threatened and even submerged by the constant demands of others.

We may be justified in our particular complaints. Our husbands, parents, children, or fellow Christians may make unreasonable demands on us. But grudging service on our part does not only make life miserable for them but can also sour our own happiness and spoil our witness. The Master said, 'I am among you as one who serves.' When he washed the disciples' feet he showed us the spirit in which to take on the most ordinary and everyday jobs for others. 'I have given you this as an example that you should do as I have done. Believe me, the servant is not greater than his master . . . Once you have realized these things, you will find your happiness in doing them.'

The Elixir

Teach me, my God and King,
In all things thee to see,
And what I do in anything,
To do it as for thee:

All may of thee partake:
Nothing can be so mean,
Which with this tincture, 'for thy sake',
Will not grow bright and clean.

A servant with this clause
Makes drudgery divine:
Who sweeps a room, as for thy laws,
Makes that and the action fine.

This is the famous stone
That turneth all to gold:
For that which God doth touch and own
Cannot for less be told.

George Herbert 1593-1632

Fill us, we pray thee, with thy light and life, that we may show forth thy wondrous glory. Grant that thy love may so fill our lives that we may count nothing too small to do for thee, nothing too much to give, and nothing too hard to bear. So teach us, Lord, to serve thee as thou deservest, to give and not to count the cost, to fight and not to heed the wounds, to toil and not to seek for rest, to labour and not to ask for any reward save that of knowing that we do thy will. Amen.

Ignatius Loyola

Day twenty-seven

Look at the birds of the air . . . Consider the lilies of the field.
                                        Matthew 6:26, 28 RSV

On one occasion I lay ill in bed, at that low ebb when nothing seems to matter, and one has no inclination even to try to get stronger. The spring sunshine was on a big spruce, which nearly brushed the jasmine around the open bedroom window. Suddenly, two lovely little sprites (they seemed something more than mere squirrels) came lilting over the trees — I can think of no other word which better describes their graceful, light, curving leaps — and for reasons known only to themselves, they decided to remain for a while in the spruce tree. There they played at hide-and-seek, one lying flat along a half-hidden bough, waiting to pounce on the other, who was looking for him. They chased each other high and low, their coats glinting a really brilliant red in the sunshine. Then one of them came to the extreme edge of the branch nearest my window. Sitting on his hind legs, he took a spray in his front paws, and nibbled at it for a few minutes, looking all the while such a lovable morsel as he sat there, where I could watch every movement, every glance of his eyes. The sight of these fearless, happy little creatures, simply content to enjoy the things provided for them by an unknown friend, seemed to put new life into me. They did more to help me take hold once more of daily living than all the good advice and bottles of medicine in the world could ever have done.

                                        Flora Klickmann

> *I come in the little things,*
> *Saith the Lord:*
> *Not borne on morning wings*
> *Of majesty, but I have set My Feet*
> *Amidst the delicate and bladed wheat*
> *That springs triumphant in the furrowed sod.*
> *There do I dwell, in weakness and in power;*
> *Not broken or divided, saith our God!*
> *In your strait garden plot I come to flower:*
> *About your porch My Vine*
> *Meek, fruitful, doth entwine;*
> *Waits, at the threshold, love's appointed hour.*

I come in the little things,
Saith the Lord:
Yea, on the glancing wings
Of eager birds, the softly pattering feet
Of furred and gentle beasts, I come to meet
Your hard and wayward heart. In brown bright eyes
That peep out from the brake, I stand confest.
On every nest
Where feathery Patience is content to brood
And leaves her pleasure for the high emprize
Of motherhood —
There doth My Godhead rest.

I come in the little things,
Saith the Lord:
My starry wings
I do forsake,
Love's highway of humility to take:
Meekly I fit my stature to your need.
In beggar's part
About your gates I shall not cease to plead —
As man, to speak with man —
Till by such art
I shall achieve My Immemorial Plan,
Pass the low lintel of the human heart.

Evelyn Underhill

Thank you, Lord, for the loveliness and the infinite variety of all your creation. Thank you for the beauty of gardens and countryside, for the pleasure of watching wild creatures and the joy of our pet animals.

Speak to me today through the things you have made. Help me to understand your greatness, your loving kindness and your constant care as I consider the works of your hands. For Jesus' sake.   Amen.

Day twenty-eight

It is full time now for you to wake from sleep. For salvation is nearer to us now than when we first believed; the night is far gone, the day is at hand.

Romans 13:11-12 RSV

Sloth, we may confidently affirm, is *not* a sin into which we are likely to fall. Aren't we always being told that we don't sit down for a minute? There just aren't enough hours in the day for all the things we have to do. The proverbial picture of the sluggard is of one who is all in favour of a little more 'folding of the hands'.

But if we look at the virtue which was set in contrast to sloth we shall find that it is not 'busyness' but watchfulness. In the Garden of Gethsemane the Master's word to the sleepy disciples was to 'watch'. The Christians of a bygone age had the sense to realize, as we often do not, that sloth is not physical inactivity but the failure to be spiritually equipped and prepared.

In Matthew's Gospel (24:42; 25:10) our Lord repeats the injunction to watch and illustrates the meaning of the command by means of several parables. Watchfulness presupposes a person or event to be watched for — the coming of the Lord himself. The slothful servant in the parables is one who leads a life of self-indulgence (eats and drinks with the drunken) and who fails to care for the needs of others — material and spiritual (begins to beat his fellow-servants). He is also one who fails to use to the full the gifts and resources given to him by God (I hid your talent).

We may be thoroughly busy people with meetings most evenings and yet be guilty of sloth because we are not watching for the Lord by using our time and energies with his coming in mind. The quality of our life rather than the quantity of activity is the true criterion of watchfulness.

'It is time to wake up to reality. Every day brings God's salvation nearer. The night is nearly over, the day has almost dawned. Let us therefore fling away the things that men do in the dark, let us arm ourselves for the fight of the day! . . . Let us be Christ's men from head to foot and give no chances to the flesh to have its fling' (Rom. 13:11-14 Phillips).

At the round earth's imagined corners, blow
Your trumpets, angels, and arise, arise
From death, you numberless infinities
Of souls, and to your scattered bodies go,
All whom the flood did, and fire shall o'erthrow,
All whom war, dearth, age, agues, tyrannies,
Despair, law, chance, hath slain, and you whose eyes
Shall behold God, and never taste death's woe.
But let them sleep, Lord, and me mourn a space,
For if above all these my sins abound,
'Tis late to ask abundance of thy grace
When we are there; here on this holy ground
Teach me how to repent; for that's as good
As if thou'dst sealed my pardon with thy blood.

John Donne 1572-1631

Make us, we beseech thee, O Lord our God, watchful in awaiting the coming of thy Son, Christ our Lord; that when he shall come and knock, he may find us not sleeping in sin, but awake, and rejoicing in his praises; through the same Jesus Christ our Lord.　Amen.

Bright's　*Ancient Collects*

c

Marriage

For this reason a man shall leave his father and mother and be joined to his wife, and the two shall become one. So they are no longer two but one.

Mark 10:7-8 RSV

Leave father and mother
At my own wedding the late Harold St John explained that if a woman put her love for the man she is to marry in one pan of the scales and her love for parents, relatives and friends in the other, the scales would come down in his favour — such is her love for him. And such should be the priority of husband or wife over all others.

Be joined to his wife
Marriage is togetherness in every sense. There should be no withholding from each other, no keeping at arm's length, no secrets, no reserve. Instead we should share every part of ourselves, body, mind and spirit. Anything that comes between must be dealt with quickly.

The two become one
Our Lord underlined this phrase by adding, 'so they are no longer two but one'. In marriage we present a united front to the world. Parents, friends, neighbours — all should know that no disloyal word will be spoken by one of the other. Children must learn that what one parent says the other will support, so that they can't drive a wedge between us. Decisions will be made together. How we spend money or use our home, how we bring up the children, will be matters to talk and pray about together.

Making each other top priority, practising togetherness, being one in everything — how easy and natural it seems at the outset of a marriage! Yet because we are all by nature selfish and often unloving, we are going to need God's grace and the love he can give if we are to achieve his pattern for marriage. And as he does help and enrich our marriage, those around may catch a glimpse of the wonderful relationship between ourselves and Christ, for in Paul's words: 'The marriage relationship is doubtless a great mystery, but I'm speaking of something deeper still — the marriage of Christ and his church' (Eph. 5:32 Phillips).

A Psalm for Marriage

I am married, I am married, and my heart is glad.
I will give thanks unto the Lord for the love and protection of my husband. I will give thanks for the blessed protection and satisfaction of my home. I will give thanks that I have someone of my own to help and comfort and even to worry about, someone to encourage and to love.

My husband is beside me wherever I need to go. My husband is behind me supporting me in whatever I need to do. I need not face the world alone. I need not face my family alone.

I need face only myself and my God alone. And this is good. This is very good.

Whatever our differences, whatever our trials, I will give thanks unto the Lord for my husband and my marriage. For so long as I have both my husband and my God I am a woman complete. I am not alone.

Marjorie Holmes   Lord, Let Me Love

Father, all good things come from you. Thank you for your gift of marriage.
We ask your loving help for those beginning married life. Give them understanding and thought for each other. Keep them trusting and loyal.
Some of us have been married many years. Forgive us if we have come to take each other for granted. Refresh and restore the love and tenderness we may have lost.
Come into our homes and rule there as Lord.   Amen.

The birth of a baby

For this child I prayed; and the Lord has granted me my petition which I made to him.

1 Samuel 1:27 RSV

How can I express the thrill of seeing our firstborn hung aloft by his heels? Of seeing his little purple body flush red? Of hearing a wonderfully strong and deep first cry? There are no words for the waves of joy, relief, and gratitude that surged over me. A son!

As we examined our little boy a few minutes later — observing his straight little nose, his ears exactly like Cam's, his tiny hands perfect replicas of Grandpa Hancock's — our hearts swelled with worship to a Creator who could so marvellously make a child, and make him ours. There in the hospital room, Cam held his son in his arms and together we presented our child to our heavenly Father, asking that his life would bring only glory to God's name. How earnestly we prayed that our wonderful, beautiful little Son of Adam would early, early, become a son of God.

And then Cam was gone, and the baby was gone, and there was rest — deep, sweet rest — for a girl who had, in a wonderful, exultant moment, become a mother.

In those first few days, I had sweet communion with the Lord as he taught me, through this new and profound experience, more about himself. There were new analogies for me to understand. As I realized how deep was our love for a tiny, helpless infant who had done nothing to deserve our love at all, except to be born into our family, I had a new realization of God's Father love for us, his sons — entirely undeserved, but ours simply because we are his sons!

How new and real became our Lord Jesus Christ's condescension in incarnation. That the great Creator could become the weakest and most helpless of his creatures . . . God — in the womb; God — at the breast; God — in nappies!

And then, one morning, as I 'kept all these things and pondered them in my heart', my heart suddenly overflowed with praise for the whole manner of birth, the whole beautiful pattern. 'Trust God,' I thought, 'to plan such a beautiful way to continue the human race. Trust God to plan that a child should be the result and fruit of love. And thank God he made me a Woman!'

Maxine Hancock   Love, Honour and be Free

Give heed, my heart, lift up thine eyes:
Who is it in yon manger lies?
Who is this child so young and fair?
The blessed Christ Child lieth there.

Ah, Lord, who has created all,
How hast thou made thee weak and small,
That thou must choose thy infant bed
Where ox and ass but lately fed?

Ah, dearest Jesus, holy Child,
Make thee a bed, soft, undefiled,
Within my heart, that it may be
A quiet chamber kept for thee.

Martin Luther 1483-1546
(Trans. Catherine Winkworth)

Lord, we are bringing a new child home to our family.
    We drive past familiar, busy streets,
        people walking by
        en route to work, to the shops,
        all of them involved in lives of great variety:
    This baby in my arms will be one of them some day.
    What will the world hold then?
Dear God, bless this little child.
    Touch this small one's life
        with love, with beauty
        and a sense of the wonder of living
        and of other people.
Help us care and give — endowing each family member
        with love and protection
        and a personal sense of importance,
    so that every child is strong,
        able to fit into that future world
        and to appreciate life.
I'm crying — the responsibility is so huge!
    And the promise is so beautiful.

Judith Mattison   *Prayers from a Mother's Heart*

Moving home

The place God has assigned for the woman is the husband's home. Most people have forgotten nowadays what a home can mean, though some of us have come to realize it as never before. It is a kingdom of its own in the midst of the world, a haven of refuge amid the turmoil of our age, nay more, a sanctuary. It is not founded on the shifting sands of private and public life, but has its peace in God. For it is God who gave it its special meaning and dignity, its nature and privilege, its destiny and worth. It is an ordinance God has established in the world, the place where peace, quietness, joy, love, purity, continence, respect, obedience, tradition, and, to crown them all, happiness may dwell, whatever else may pass away in the world. It is the woman's calling and her joy to build up this world within the world for her husband, and to make it the scene of her activity. How happy she is when she realizes what a noble and rich destiny and task is hers. Not novelty, but permanence, not change, but constancy, not noisiness, but peace, not words, but deeds, not peremptoriness, but persuasion, and all these things inspired and sustained by her love for her husband — such is the woman's kingdom.

Dietrich Bonhoeffer
(A Wedding Sermon from a Prison Cell)

Lord, here is our new home. Please come in and make it *your* home. Live here as you live in our hearts as owner and master. May your peace and your love be felt in these rooms. Give us your rest. May all who come inside these doors sense your presence here. Make this new house a home. To your glory.   Amen.

Ah, Father! A moment's rest.
I must sit for a while before going to bed
in our new home.
I'm exhausted, Lord.
I haven't realized what a strain
these past weeks have been.
There was so much to pack and discard!
How did we accumulate so many things?
And there is so much left to do:
curtains to make,
walls to paint,
unpacking and arranging,
new shops,
new neighbours,
a new address,
new problems.
But I will try to take it all a day at a time.
Father, help us.
As we begin this new segment of our life,
watch us,
guide us,
and help us in whatever needs we have,
Thank you for this opportunity.

Judith Mattison
Prayers from a Mother's Heart

Lord, here I am, alone in my new home. Help me to welcome inside
my door not only my old friends and good neighbours but also
the lonely
the sad
those whose own homes are broken or unhappy.
Teach me the art of home-making so that others may find comfort,
peace and happiness here. For Jesus' sake.   Amen.

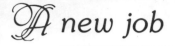# A new job

I told them how God had been with me and helped me . . . And they got ready to start the work.

Nehemiah 2:18 TEV

Even if Potiphar paid thirty or even forty pieces of silver for his Hebrew slave, we know now what a good bargain he got that day. For that handful of silver the captain of Pharaoh's guard came into possession of all the splendid talents that lay hid in Joseph's greatly gifted mind, and all the magnificent moral character the first foundations of which had been laid in the pit in Dothan, and had been built up in God every step of the long wilderness journey. All Joseph's deep repentance also, and all his bitter remorse; all his self-discovery, and all his self-condemnation; with all his reticence and all his continence — Potiphar took all that home from the slave-market that day in exchange for his handful of Egyptian silver. Joseph was now to be plunged into the most corrupt society that rotted in that age on the face of the earth. And had he not come into that pollution straight out of a sevenfold furnace of sanctifying sorrow, Joseph would no more have been heard of. The sensuality of Egypt would have soon swallowed him up. But his father's God was with Joseph. The Lord was with Joseph to protect him, to guide him, and to give him the victory. The Lord was with him to more imprisonment, and then to more promotion; to more and more honour, and place, and power, till this world had no more to bestow upon Joseph. And, through it all, Joseph became a better and an ever better man all his days. A nobler and an ever nobler man. A more and more trustworthy, and a more and more trusted and consulted man. More and more loyal to truth and to duty. More and more chaste, temperate, patient, enduring, forgiving; full of mind and full of heart; and full, no man ever fuller, of a simple and a sincere piety and praise of God, till he became a very proverb both in the splendour of his services, and in the splendour of his rewards.

Alexander Whyte   *Bible Characters*

Lord, look upon our working day,
Busied in factory, office, store;
May wordless work your name adore,
The common round spell out your praise.

You are the workman, Lord, not we:
All worlds were made at your command,
Christ, their sustainer, bared his hand,
Retrieved them from futility.

Our part to do what he'll commit,
Who strides the world, and calls men all
Partners in pain and carnival,
To grasp the hope he won for it.

Ian M Fraser 1917-

O God, this is a special day for me, and I need your help;
I cannot guess what this day will hold for me; I do not even know
with whom I shall work.

> Quicken my brain today, I pray, and guide my hand.
> Let me do well what is required of me.
> Let me not excuse myself for any fault that appears.

O God, remind me to be prompt, and courteous, this day.
Let me work as carefully when no one sees, as at any time.
Enable me to co-operate with my fellow-workers, I pray.

You have put into our hands the joy of creation;
You have made us able to make things good and beautiful;
You have challenged us to choose lasting values.   Amen.

Rita Snowden   *Prayers for Busy People*

 birthday

This is the day which the Lord has made; let us rejoice and be glad in it.
Psalm 118: 24 RSV

We say: When I get married . . .

               When we move into a new house . . .

               When the children start school . . .

               When I haven't the old folk to look after . . .

Have you ever thought how much time and energy we spend longing for some time in the near or distant future when we think that life will really begin, or that circumstances will be more congenial? Sometimes we are planning to enjoy ourselves without some of the ties and difficulties that make present life a burden. Sometimes we may genuinely be looking forward to a time when we think we shall be able to serve God more actively. Whatever our motive, we're waiting for the future in order to live.

Almost without realizing it, we may reach the top of the hill and with it the goal we had sighted afar off. No sooner have we done so than we turn about and begin to look in the opposite direction. Having waited years to get the children or the old folk off our hands, we are already talking nostalgically of the days when they were with us.

We say: When the children were small . . .

               When I was out at work . . .

               When we used to have the young people around . . .

               When we lived at the other house . . .

It seems as if our chance of living a full and satisfying life has slipped through our fingers along with those responsibilities we once waited to escape from. Those were the days!

Left to ourselves it is only too easy to squander time either by longing for the future or dreaming of the past. The Bible teaches us to use today. God does not hold us responsible for the past — which he has forgiven — or for the future — which he has not yet given to us — but for the present. We can give today to God and he can use us in it as he can use us at no other time. And however we may have changed during the years that have passed we can be sure that the One who travels with us never changes. He is that wonderful Lord who kept faith with us in the past and who awaits us in the unknown future. He is the same yesterday, today and for ever.

Now thank we all our God,
With heart and hands and voices,
Who wondrous things hath done,
In whom his world rejoices;
Who from our mother's arms
Hath blessed us on our way
With countless gifts of love,
And still is ours today.

O may this bounteous God
Through all our life be near us,
With ever joyful hearts
And blessed peace to cheer us;
And keep us in his grace,
And guide us when perplexed,
And free us from all ills
In this world and the next.

All praise and thanks to God
The Father now be given,
The Son, and him who reigns
With them in highest heaven;
The One eternal God,
Whom earth and heaven adore;
For thus it was, is now,
And shall be evermore.

Martin Rinkart 1586-1649, tr. Catherine Winkworth

Father, we come to you on this birthday to thank you for all your help and love in the year that has passed. Thank you for the kindness of family and friends received today. Now we look ahead to another year. We believe that all it will contain is known to you and will be for our good. Help us now to use the present to the full and to serve you and to help others. For Jesus' sake.   Amen.

Retirement

*I am your God and will take care of you until you are old and your
hair is grey. I made you and will care for you; I will give you help.*
Isaiah 46:4 TEV

One other way in which we can prepare for retirement is by
cultivating a love of solitude. This cannot be done overnight and
must be started much earlier in life. There are some who live their
lives in a whirl of frenzied activism and keep this up till the last of the
retirement dinners is over. Retirement for them must be hard and
perhaps only possible at first with the aid of tranquillisers. However,
to have developed a love of outward solitude that leads to inner
solitude which in turn frees us from the distraction of ourselves and
other people for God is a most valuable lesson. We can begin to
practise this at an early age, and the younger the better, by
disciplining ourselves. When we find ourselves alone for an evening,
what do we do?

Rush around to our nearest friend to spend the evening together
with *someone*?

Get on to the phone for long conversations?

Busy ourselves with non-essential household chores?

But why not stay alone and simply be still?

Maybe listen to a little music?

Do some quiet reflecting on life?

Remember friends we have scarcely had time to think of in the
weeks of busyness?

Enjoy having the cat on our lap, or the dog on the mat in front of
us?

Look at (not just glance at) the paintings on the wall that we by-
pass every day in our hurry and see in them again the qualities that
attracted us in the first place?

If we have built up a cosy little home, then why not just sit in it
(quite still) and enjoy it? Have you ever had a lengthy period of
illness when you have lain in one room? By the end of the illness you
know every detail of the room and the shape of the trees out of the
window and the different parts of the pictures on the wall that are
highlighted by the sun at different times of the day. Lying there, you
may have reached some pretty clear thoughts about life, its meaning,
its purpose and *your* place in the scheme of things. Eventually you
emerge from bed, weaker and thinner maybe, but with a clearer

perspective and a sense that this suffering had been creative. But why do we need to wait until we are ill to experience this quality of life? Solitude is something for which we should make time regularly, learning to enjoy it and the heightened awareness that comes with it. Through it too, we can learn to enjoy the companionship of God whose resources are as adequate to meet the needs of our retirement as they have been during our working lives.

Margaret Evening   *Who Walk Alone*

Dismiss me not thy service, Lord,
But train me for thy will;
For even I, in fields so broad,
Some duties may fulfil;
And I will ask for no reward,
Except to serve thee still.

All works are good, and each is best
As it most pleases thee;
Each worker pleases when the rest
He serves in charity;
And neither man nor work unblest
Wilt thou permit to be

Our Master all the work has done
He asks of us today;
Sharing his service, every one
Share too his Sonship may;
Lord, I would serve and be a son;
Dismiss me not, I pray.

Thomas Toke Lynch 1818-71

Lord, meet us now in this new chapter of life. Calm our fears. Supply our needs.

Save us from making the days of retirement overbusy. We would take time to be still, to hear you speak to us and to listen to others.

Save us too from becoming self-pitying or self-indulgent. Teach us that our work for you will never end. We are your servants still until the day when we shall serve you night and day in perfect happiness in the kingdom of our Lord Jesus Christ.   Amen.

Personal loss

I will not leave you desolate; I will come to you.

John 14:18 RSV

I didn't question God's wisdom in allowing Jeff's death. I no longer tormented myself with recriminations for my own actions, nor did I batter heaven with my prayers for acceptance of the situation. I accepted the inevitable, and, during the day, managed to do it with a fairly good grace. It was at night that this frightening and empty loneliness hit me — frightening because of the enormous responsibilities that I now had to carry, and empty because I had to carry them alone.

The conflict was once more inside me. I knew that God had made promises that covered all the situations in which I found myself, and I was still convinced that 'All things work together for good to them that love God', but this knowledge and this conviction did not prevent the emotions raging in my mind.

Now I was like a beetle lying on its back scrabbling with its feet in the air, wanting to turn over but not knowing how. I couldn't pray or read my Bible and when I tried it seemed that I grasped thin air. There seemed no reality beyond, yet deep down I knew that God was there. His love and his power still surrounded me. Because I didn't *feel* anything spiritually it didn't mean that God had deserted me. Once my emotions had touched rock-bottom I began to surface again spiritually. It was as if I had to be thrown flat on my back with all my tenderest feelings exposed before I was able to put my feet on the support that God was offering me and be turned up the right way again. My friends had supported me for a time in prayer, but now it was God's turn to take over completely. Only after I had relaxed sufficiently to allow the tears free rein did I find I could talk to God with, if anything, more intimacy than before. Through my weakness I found his power.

Jenny Chadwick   *Without Jeff*

I know that my Redeemer lives:
What comfort this sweet sentence gives!
He lives, he lives who once was dead;
He lives, my everlasting Head.

He lives, my kind, wise, constant Friend;
Who still will keep me to the end;
He lives, and while he lives I'll sing,
Jesus, my Prophet, Priest, and King.

Samuel Medley 1738-99

Help me, Lord Jesus,
    to accept you as my Way,
    to hear your voice
        and to follow you,
    to learn right attitudes to the future as well as the past.

Guide me in the decisions which
    will have to be made.

Deliver me from any self-pity or hopelessness
    and give me courage to live as fully as I can
    for your glory.

Thank you Lord.   Amen.

For the Funeral Day
Lord Jesus Christ I come to you at the beginning of this day;
    in all my loneliness and uncertainty I come.
I thank you for all those who will be
    sharing the day with me,
    for the minister, relatives and friends,
        and all those who have been so helpful.

Help me not to worry
    about the arrangements that have been made,
    about the visitors who will be coming,
    about my fear of emotion,
        about the service, the weather.

I bring this day to you;
    help me in my weakness
        to prove your strength.   Amen.

Comforting others

Praise be to the God and Father of our Lord Jesus Christ, the Father of compassion and the God of all comfort, who comforts us in all our troubles, so that we can comfort those in any trouble with the comfort we ourselves have received from God.

2 Corinthians 1:3-4 NIV

'When Job's friends came to see him after his children died and he had suffered in so many ways,' suggests a friend of mine who is a psychiatrist, 'they missed the opportunity to go down in history as uniquely sensitive and understanding. There they sat on the ground with him for seven days and nights, and they didn't say a word, because they saw how utterly grief-stricken he was. But then they began to talk and spoiled it all.'

Sensitivity in the presence of grief should usually make us more silent, more listening. 'I'm sorry' is honest: 'I know how you feel' is usually not — even though you may have experienced the death of a person who had the same familial relationship to you as the deceased person had to the grieving one.

If the person feels that you can understand, he'll tell you. Then you may want to share your own honest, not prettied-up feelings in your personal aftermath with death. Don't try to 'prove' anything to a survivor. An arm about the shoulder, a firm grip on the hand, a kiss: these are the proofs grief needs, not logical reasoning. I was sitting, torn by grief. Someone came and talked to me of God's dealings, of why it happened, of hope beyond the grave. He talked constantly, he said things I knew were true.

I was unmoved, except to wish he'd go away. He finally did.

Another came and sat beside me. He didn't talk. He didn't ask leading questions. He just sat beside me for an hour and more, listened when I said something, answered briefly, prayed simply, left.

I was moved. I was comforted. I hated to see him go.

Joseph Bayly   *The Last Thing We Talk About*

Help me, dear Lord, to find some heart that's broken,
Some life where faith and hope are burning low:
Help me to speak the word that should be spoken,
That they thy love and saving power may know.

Lord, make me an instrument of thy peace.
Where there is hatred, let me sow love;
Where there is injury, pardon;
Where there is doubt, faith;
Where there is despair, hope,
Where there is darkness, light;
Where there is sadness, joy.

O Divine Master, grant that
I may not so much seek
To be consoled, as to console;
Not so much to be understood as
To understand; not so much to be
Loved as to love:
For it is in giving that we receive;
It is in pardoning, that we are pardoned;
It is in dying, that we awaken to eternal life.

St Francis of Assisi

Family quarrels

Be kind to one another, tenderhearted, forgiving one another, as God in Christ forgave you.

Ephesians 4:32 RSV

Never go to bed angry.

Ephesians 4:26 Phillips

It may be an infinitely less evil to murder a man than to refuse to forgive him. The former may be the act of a moment of passion: the latter is the heart's choice.

No man who will not forgive his neighbour, can believe that God is willing, yea wanting, to forgive *him* . . . If God said, 'I forgive you' to a man who hated his brother, and if (as is impossible) that voice of forgiveness should reach the man, what would it mean to him? How would the man interpret it? Would it not mean to him 'You may go on hating. I do not mind it. You have had great provocation and are justified in your hate'? No doubt God takes what wrong there is, and what provocation there is, into the account: but the more the provocation, the more excuse that can be urged for the hate, the more reason, if possible, that the hater should be delivered from the hell of his hate . . . The man would think, not that God loved the sinner, but that he forgave the sin, which God never does . . . He loves the sinner so much that he cannot forgive him in any other way than by banishing from his bosom the demon that possesses him.

George Macdonald   *An Anthology* by C S Lewis

There is no use talking as if forgiveness were easy. We all know the old joke, 'You've given up smoking once; I've given it up a dozen times.' In the same way I could say of a certain man, 'Have I forgiven him for what he did that day? I've forgiven him more times than I can count.' For we find that the work of forgiveness has to be done over and over again. We forgive, we mortify our resentment; a week later some chain of thought carries us back to the original offence and we discover the old resentment blazing away as if nothing had been done about it at all. We need to forgive our brother seventy times seven not only for 490 offences but for one offence.

C S Lewis   *Reflections on the Psalms*

Dear Lord and Father of mankind,
Forgive our foolish ways!
Re-clothe us in our rightful mind:
In purer lives thy service find,
In deeper reverence, praise.

Drop thy still dews of quietness
Till all our strivings cease:
Take from our souls the strain and stress,
And let our ordered lives confess
The beauty of thy peace.

Breathe through the heats of our desire
Thy coolness and thy balm;
Let sense be dumb — let flesh retire,
Speak through the earthquake, wind, and fire,
O still small voice of calm!

John Greenleaf Whittier 1807-92

Dear Lord Jesus, we have quarrelled and nothing can undo the things we've said and done. I am frightened and ashamed of the hatred and bitterness I felt — now I am numbed and unhappy. Please forgive me for my share in the quarrel. I know you can only do that as I forgive the person who wronged me — so make me willing to forgive and show me how.

Lord, I pray for your healing. There are wounds that hurt and there is distance and hostility where there should be closeness and understanding. Please bring us near to you and to each other, making peace through the blood of your cross.   Amen.

Going into hospital

Don't worry over anything whatever; tell God every detail of your needs in earnest and thankful prayer, and the peace of God, which transcends human understanding, will keep constant guard over your hearts and minds as they rest in Christ Jesus.

Philippians 4:6-7 Phillips

Don't worry, the apostle begins, in typically masculine fashion we may feel. But as we read on we find step by step instructions for putting that oft-repeated advice into action.

Tell God every detail of your needs may sound a truism. We take it for granted that every Christian prays about problems and this is probably true of the ones we are fully aware of. But our worries often lurk in a twilight zone, nagging at us, weighing us down, yet barely formulated in our own minds, let alone spoken in specific detail. We must drag them into the open and tell God every worrying possibility, every puzzling alternative. *Every detail* includes those little items that can loom so large, especially as we lie awake at nights. Our prayer is to be *earnest,* a purposeful asking in order to receive, so that the intricacies of our everyday living may be patterned by God to his glory and to the blessing of the people among whom we live.

Our prayer is also to be *thankful.* In our worries we always look on the black side — we fear the worst. As we pray thankfully we not only recall God's love and his purposes of good towards us, but we bring to mind the countless past occasions on which he has cared and brought us through our difficulties. Such reminders make us confident in the present crisis.

Having turned our worries thus into prayer, we can claim the promise that follows. The peace of God will be ours. The Philippians were used to the sight of a Roman soldier on sentry duty and could have pictured God's peace as Paul describes it here, guarding heart and mind, that is both our feelings and our thoughts, from the destructive attacks of worry. His peace prevents the invasion of hostile fears all the while that we, for our part, rest those hearts and minds in child-like, loving trust on Christ Jesus our Lord.

Home

O God, my Father, all manner of questions arise in my mind just now. I suddenly know I can't manage alone — I need some help. Guide my family, my friends, my doctor.

If I have to go into hospital, keep me calm at the prospect;
if the ambulance must convey me there, sustain my courage;
if I am faced with unfamiliar routines, help me to co-operate.

I know that distance has no meaning in your loving concern — I cannot slip beyond your reach, in health or sickness. And this gives me immense support, if I must move into a strange setting.

Be specially near to all involved in this experience with me;
I can't guess what will be required, but you know;
I can't measure my strength, but you can.

You enabled Jesus to heal, when he was on earth; and you help others to do the same today. In homes, and in hospitals, you are at work, to bring us again to health. I trust you. Amen.

Rita Snowden   *When My Visitors Go*

Hospital

Thank you, O God,
for all the people who have looked after me today;
for all those who visited me today;
for the letters and the get-well cards; for the flowers and gifts friends have sent.

I know that sleep
is one of the best medicines for both the body and the mind.
Help me to sleep tonight.

Into your strong hands I place
all the patients in this ward;
the night staff on duty tonight;
my loved ones whose names I now mention;
myself, with my fears, my worries and my hopes.

Help me to sleep, thinking of you and your promises. Amen.

Visitors

I was a stranger and you received me in your homes.
When Lord?
Whenever you did this for one of the least important of these
brothers of mine, you did it for me!

Matthew 25:35,37,40 TEV

'I'm sorry really that we didn't ask him in, but you know how it is. I'd completely forgotten the time with that wonderful Bible study he'd been giving us and it was late when we got into Emmaus and I remembered that we hadn't any food left in the place except half a loaf left over from the week before. The wife looked as though she was starting one of her headaches and I wanted an early night since I really didn't know where to start with all the work that had piled up over the holiday. But anyway it was all right, he saw things were a bit tricky and he didn't offer to come in. But I did give him our address and I do hope he'll drop in next time he's passing.'

Andrew Guyatt

Yet if his Majesty, our Sovereign Lord,
Should of his own accord
Friendly himself invite,
And say, 'I'll be your guest to-morrow night,'
How should we stir ourselves, call and command
All hands to work: Let no man idle stand!

'Set me fine Spanish tables in the hall;
See they are fitted all;
Let there be room to eat
And order taken that there want no meat.
See every sconce and candlestick made bright,
That without tapers they may give a light.

Look to the presence: are the carpets spread,
The dazie o'er the head,
The cushions in the chairs,
And all the candles lighted on the stairs?
Perfume the chambers, and in any case
Let each man give attendance in his place!'

Thus, if a king were coming would we do;
And 'twere good reason too;
For 'tis a duteous thing
To show all honour to an earthly king,
And after all our travail and our cost,
So he be pleased, to think no labour lost.

But at the coming of the King of Heaven
All's set at six and seven;
We wallow in our sin,
Christ cannot find a chamber in the inn.
We entertain him always like a stranger,
And, as at first, still lodge him in the manger.

Anon.   From a Christ Church MS

Lord, visitors are coming and I'm worried. There is so much to do —
the house to clean, beds to make, meals to prepare.
And I am nervous — afraid I won't think of the right things to say or
that the house won't look good enough. Help me to think instead of
how *they* are feeling. I can forget myself in making them feel at ease.
Show me how to welcome them into our home so that they can relax
and sense that they are wanted for their own sake. So make their
stay a blessing to us all.   Amen

Lord, bless our unexpected visitors.
Those who call:
>   when we'd planned an evening on our own
>   when we are watching a special TV programme
>   when I'd decided to wash my hair
>   when the family wants me
>   when I'm up to my eyes in work.

Never let me turn them away or subtly get across the message
that they are not wanted.
Remind me that in welcoming them into my home I am welcoming you.   Amen.

When I have leisure

Let us go off by ourselves to some place where we will be alone and you can rest for a while.

Mark 6:31 TEV

How often this verse is quoted as endorsement by our Lord of our need for leisure. Rather wryly we recall that the disciples never had the planned rest. Instead, hours of teaching by our Lord were followed by the mammoth undertaking of the feeding of the five thousand, the exhausting all-night row back across the lake and a further full-scale healing operation. Not much leisure! But the verse does confirm the need for leisure — even though our plans to get it don't always succeed.

The trouble is that most of us are plagued by what is known as the 'protestant work ethic'. Every minute not utilized in activity is felt to be sinful waste of time. As a student I listened to a speaker telling us what a wicked waste of a Christian's time it was to read the advertisements at the front and back of a magazine. Such teaching made no allowance for the need to unwind, to alternate intensive work with periods of rest. To give no time for leisure is in fact counter-productive. We become less efficient and our work output drops.

How wisely God ordained the Sabbath rest! Yet our Sundays are often our busiest days. But if Sunday must be chockful of action, we must make time for rest on some other day. We owe it to our Creator to use body, mind and spirit effectively — and as he intended.

Then how should we spend our hard won leisure? Like everything else, our leisure belongs to God and must be planned in consultation with him and according to his laws. But other than that — whatever makes *me* unwind and relax is good for *me*. One woman's leisure may be another's hard work! Contrast with our usual working pattern is important. Those who have sedentary jobs may want exercise — the usually active may read a good book or watch television. For the stay-at-homes, an outing, and for those with a routine job something creative (baking a cake or painting a picture). Any of these — and many more activities — can bring the recreation we need. For recreation is the purpose of leisure. To re-create body, mind and spirit, so that, refreshed, we can return to the service of others to which God has called us.

Lord, let me take time for beauty.
Time for a jug of flowers on the table, or a plant if flowers
  aren't in bloom.
Time for a dab of lipstick or a fresh blouse before the
  family comes home.

You've made the world so beautiful, Lord, let me take
  time to see it. Even as I'm rushing to the market or
  driving children to their destinations, let me be aware
  of it: the glory of hills and woods and shining water.
  The colours of traffic lights and yellow buses, of fruit
  stands and lumberyards, of girls wearing bright scarves
  that dance in the breeze.

Let me take time for the beauty in my own back yard,
  Lord.

Let me lift my eyes from the dishes to rejoice in the
  sunshine spilling through the trees. In the squirrels
  darting jaunty-plumed along the bleached boards of
  the fence. In the raindrops strung out on the clothes
  line like a string of crystal beads.

Let me take time for beauty, Lord.

Marjorie Holmes   *Lord, Let Me Love*

Father, we thank you for leisure. We accept it as a gift from you. Help us to unwind and to use our leisure to become more relaxed people — better at our jobs and nicer to live with.
Help us to accept interruptions to our free time with a good grace. May we think of others' needs before our own self-pleasing. For Jesus' sake.   Amen.

When I am busy

In returning and rest you shall be saved; in quietness and trust shall be your strength.

Isaiah 30:14 RSV

At supper, when you pour the milk, you fill one glass at a time. In your daily affairs, you have to learn to fill each minute at a time, otherwise some minutes will overflow while others remain empty.

Constantly tell yourself: for this moment I have only one person to deal with, and that's the one who's right in front of me; I have only one letter to write, the one I'm writing right now; I have only one thing to do, what I'm doing here and now. In this way you'll be able to work more rapidly, more efficiently, and with a lot less headaches. Sleep and relaxation are not a waste of time. Each of us has different needs in this regard. We have to know ourselves and allot exactly the time necessary for preserving our peace of mind and ability to work. Don't take less than you need or you'll wear yourself down. Don't take more than you need or you'll become a glutton for it. Have you a lot of work to do? Offer your sleep or your leisure to the Lord and be at peace. You're not wasting your time. Time is a gift of God and he will demand of us an exact accounting of our use of it. But be at peace: God is not an overbearing father, he doesn't give us a job to do without at the same time giving us the means to accomplish it. We always have time to do what God would have us do.

When you don't have enough time to get everything done, stop for a moment and pray. Then place your work before God as you do it. What you can't finish, leave, even if others become insistent and refuse to understand, for God has not given you this work to do. You never have *too much* work to do. Once you see what God wants you to do, then leave everything else aside and put yourself completely into the task at hand. God is waiting for you here at this very moment, at this very place and nowhere else.

Michel Quoist   The Christian Response

Lord, teach me how to stand still.
To switch off; to lean on a gate;
to sit and look at your beautiful world.
Teach me how to leave the phone off,
to slacken speed, to lie in the sun without
a feeling that I should be doing something.
Teach me, Lord, to stop, to stop fussing,
To stop working at it, to stop keeping on bravely,
To stop doing it all myself ('no help
        y'know, all by myself').

Teach me, Lord, to let others help me.
Teach me to delegate, to trust.
That which I do, let's face it, is
        not so important.
Doing it alone makes me feel important.

It also makes me feel tired and
        irritable and anxious and fearful
        of what will happen if I'm off sick.
And not liking the thought that very little
        would happen; that the earth would
        not shake — and probably nobody
        would notice for a week or two.
Why can't I stop running, Lord?

Teach me, Lord, to stop, to look, and listen.
        To be still in the mind when I stop.
        To see beauty when I look.
        To hear more when I listen.

                David Kossoff   *You Have a Minute, Lord?*

Teach us to care and not to care
Teach us to sit still

                T S Eliot   *Ash Wednesday*

When one of the family is ill

Fear not, for I am with you, be not dismayed, for I am your God; I will strengthen you, I will help you, I will uphold you.

Isaiah 41:10 RSV

For many women, life is a matter of looking after others and meeting their needs. Whether single or married our own wishes and interests have very often to go by the board because of the demands of others. I wonder how we accept this exercise in unselfishness.

'I am the Lord's servant,' Mary told Gabriel. 'May it happen to me as you have said.' The way ahead was to be hard and painful yet she did not accept the high and difficult honour in any spirit of resentment or of martyrlike resignation but with willing gladness. She saw herself as the Lord's servant. 'Christ is the *real* Master you serve,' Paul reminded the Christian slaves at Colosse.

For Mary, a human being created by God, submission was a proper response. But for the Lord of glory to submit to the limitations of humanity was an act of humility so tremendous and wholly unexpected that we can hardly take it in. Having stooped to become flesh, his practice in life was 'not to be served but to serve'. He went about doing good and healing the sick. 'Even Christ pleased not himself,' Paul comments in wonder. Whether we have to run round others in a busy household or care for them when they are ill, we can offer our service as an act of love and gratitude to the Lord who 'himself bore our sicknesses and carried our pains'.

A Sick Child

Help me through those times of sickness.
When I worry, let me trust you
*   and rely on the doctor for help.*

When I am tired,
*   up all night with a whining toddler,*
*   or a child with an upset stomach,*
*   or a fitful infant,*
when the day drags on
*   rocking a little one,*
*   entertaining one half-well,*
*   cooking extra meals,*
*   washing sheets,*
*   disinfecting bathrooms,*
*   running to the clinic —*
*   keep me going, Father.*
If my vigil takes me
*   to intensive care or pediatric wards or*
*   dental surgeons,*
*   help me be calm but loving,*
*   reassuring and hopeful —*
*   believing*
*   in the Great Physician's power*
*   and abundant love.*

Heal the wounds, Lord.
*   Bless the child.*
*   Sustain the mother.*
*   Thank you, Lord.*

Judith Mattison   *Prayers from a Mother's Heart*

Lord, give me strength of body and mind to nurse this loved one
through a long illness. It is hard to keep on cheerfully day in and day
out, bearing such an extra load of work and worry. Give me
patience. Help me not to get tense or sharp-tongued.
May we all face this illness with fortitude and hope.   Amen.

When others try us

The fruit of the Spirit is . . . patience . . . gentleness.
Galatians 5:22 RSV

There will always be faults in ourselves, faults in others, which defy correction; there is nothing for it but to put up with them, till God arranges things differently. After all, it may be the best possible way of testing your patience; and without patience a man's good qualities go for very little. At the same time, you do well to pray about such inconveniences; ask God in his mercy to help you bear them calmly.

2. If you have spoken to a man once and again without bringing him to a better mind, it is a mistake to go on nagging at him; leave it all in God's hands; let his will be done, his name be glorified, in the lives of all his servants — he knows how to bring good out of evil.

Yes, you do well to cultivate patience in putting up with the shortcomings, the various disabilities of other people; only think how much they have to put up with in you! When you make such a failure of organizing your own life, how can you expect everybody else to come up to your own standards?

3. We like to have everybody around us quite perfect, but our own faults — we never seem to correct *them*. Tom, Dick and Harry must be strictly called to order, but we aren't fond of being called to order ourselves. It is always the other man that has too much rope given him — our wishes must not be thwarted; rules for everybody else, but our own liberties must not be abridged for a moment. My neighbour as myself — it is not often, is it, that we weight the scales equally?

If we were all perfect, we should give one another no crosses to bear, and that is not what God wants.

4. He will have us learn to bear the burden of one another's faults. Nobody is faultless; each has his own burden to bear, without the strength or the wit to carry it by himself; and we have got to support one another, console, help, correct, advise one another, each in his turn.

Meanwhile, there is no better test of a man's quality than when he cannot have things his own way. The occasions of sin do not overpower us, they only prove our worth.

Thomas à Kempis   *The Imitation of Christ*

Let me go gently through life, Lord, so much more gently.

Right now, calm my exasperation as I try for the third time to get that telephone operator to respond. Let me sit gently, think gently, speak gently when the connection is made. (It may not be her fault. Or she may be young and new to the job . . . or older and troubled by the very same problems I have.)

Smooth my sharp edges of person and temper and tongue. Give me gentleness in dealing with people. Strangers like this, who are human too, subject to error and hurt. And gentleness with my family . . . Not softness, no — keep me firm — but gentle of voice instead of shrill. Gentle of movement and manner and touch.

Help me to practice gentleness. In small inconveniences like this as well as large problems with those close to me. If I can just keep gentle, firm but gentle, then I'll be better able to meet life's major crises with dignity and strength.
Thank you for giving me gentleness, God.

Marjorie Holmes   *Lord, Let Me Love*

Let it be seen that with thee I have been,
Jesus, my Lord and my Saviour;
Let it be known I am truly thine own,
By all my speech and behaviour.

The pressure of responsiblity

You can throw the whole weight of your anxieties upon him, for you are his personal concern.

1 Peter 5: 7 Phillips

I think the idea of God's personal care for the individual came upon me with unexpected strength when I came to translate 1 Peter 5: 7, which reads in the Authorised Version 'casting all your care upon him; for he careth for you'. In one sense it is quite plain that God wants us to bear responsibility; it is a false religion which teaches that God wants us to be permanently immature. But there is a sense in which the conscientious and the imaginative can be overburdened. This familiar text reminded me that such over-anxiety can be 'off-loaded' on to God for each one of us is his personal concern. The 'text' is commonplace enough, perhaps too commonplace, for it was not until I had to translate it that I came to realise something of its full force. The word used for 'casting' is an almost violent word, conveying the way in which a man at the end of his tether might throw aside an intolerable burden. And the Christian is recommended to throw this humanly insupportable weight upon the only one who can bear it and at the same time to realise that God cares for him intimately as a person. 'He careth for you' is hardly strong enough and I don't know that I did much better in rendering the words 'you are his personal concern'. The Greek words certainly mean this but probably more. It is not the least glory of the Christian gospel that the God revealed by Jesus Christ possesses wisdom and power beyond all human imagining but never loses sight of any individual human being. It may seem strange to us and it may seem an idea quite beyond our little minds to comprehend, but each one of us *matters* to God. It is of course the same sense of intimate concern which Jesus expressed poetically when he assured us that even the hairs on our head are numbered. It is the kind of inspired truth of which we have continually to remind ourselves, if only because life so often apparently contradicts it.

J B Phillips   *Ring of Truth*

Come, heavy souls, oppressed that are
With doubts, and fears, and carking care.
Lay all your burthens down, and see
Where's One that carried once a tree
Upon his back, and, which is more,
A heavier weight, your sins, he bore.
Think then how easily he can
Your sorrows bear that's God and Man;
Think too how willing he's to take
Your care on him, who for your sake
Sweat bloody drops, prayed, fasted, cried,
Was bound, scourged, mocked and crucified.
He that so much for you did do,
Will do yet more, and care for you.

Thomas Washbourne 1606-87
Oxford Book of Christian Verse

Into the hands that were wounded to save me,
Into the hands that are mighty to keep,
Into the hands that can guide me and guard me,
Saviour, my life I yield.

When money is scarce

Jesus said, 'Do not be anxious, saying, "What shall we eat?" or "What shall we drink?" or "What shall we wear?" . . . seek first his kingdom and his righteousness, and all these things shall be yours as well.'

Matthew 6:31, 33 RSV

I was no longer working on the night shift. A chance had come along for me to train at a Government Centre as a precision grinder. I had hopes of getting a steady job with better earnings — as indeed became the case for a short while. What no one had foreseen was the 'slump' of the early 1960s. The firm which took me on was one of the first to fall a victim, and I was thrown out of work and onto the dole queue, an unpleasant experience for a man with a newly acquired skill at his fingertips.

Doris was wonderful, as always.

'You'll soon get another job, don't worry. The Lord won't let us starve!' But as the weeks went by and the last date allowd for dole payment drew nearer, it began to look very much as though he might. I tried for job after job without success. As my few savings dwindled frighteningly I knew myself to be too old at fifty-one. My training had been wasted, and with my background nobody wanted to give me a trial, let alone a permanent job.

It was a real testing time. I wrestled with despair and doubt as I had done before, and again, clear and strong, I heard the Lord saying 'trust me'.

'Lord,' I prayed, 'show me what you want me to do, and I'll do it — *whatever* it is.'

The answer was so unexpected that I almost laughed.

'Go and sell some eggs,' a voice said in my head, as clear as a friend speaking.

I was a skilled workman, now, wasn't I? Surely the Lord could find me something more in line with my new status? Still, I had promised.

So off I went to the packing station and got a few dozen eggs 'on tick'; then I made for the nearest suburb and began to knock on doors.

I soon found housewives who were glad to have such a fragile item as eggs delivered to their doors, and I quickly built up a small round and paid off my debt at the packing station.

As well as getting fresh supplies of eggs, I put aside some of the profits to buy a stock of little leaflets — tracts — with a short Bible message or an inspiring thought or verse. Sometimes a customer would look surprised at being handed one of these with her eggs; usually they got stuck behind the kitchen clock, but I went on giving them out to each woman, trusting that one day the Lord would speak to someone through the simple printed words.

Fred Lemon with Gladys Knowlton *Breakout*

The God of love my shepherd is,
  And he that doth me feed:
While he is mine, and I am his,
  What can I want or need?

He leads me to the tender grass,
  Where I both feed and rest;
Then to the streams that gently pass:
  In both I have the best.

Or if I stray, he doth convert
  And bring my mind in frame:
And all this not for my desert,
  But for his holy name.

Yea, in death's shady black abode
  Well may I walk, not fear:
For thou art with me; and thy rod
  To guide, thy staff to bear.

Nay, thou dost make me sit and dine,
  Ev'n in my enemies' sight:
My head with oil, my cup with wine
  Runs over day and night.

Surely thy sweet and wondrous love
  Shall measure all my days;
And as it never shall remove,
  So neither shall my praise.

George Herbert 1593-1633

Lord, you have never failed us in the past and you have told us not to worry about the future. But you taught us to pray, 'Give us this day our daily bread.'
So we bring you our needs for today. Please meet them in your own way. Amen.

Illness of body

This illness . . . is for the glory of God, so that the Son of God may be glorified by means of it.

John 11:4 RSV

What can illness teach you about God? It will teach you not to worry any more. You will learn to leave to the Father, in his love, to decide what is best for you, both today and tomorrow.

It will teach you to be dependent upon Jesus, who in illness is your only help. Only he can turn sickness into health.

It wants to teach you the mightiest prayer, which is highly honoured in heaven: 'My Father, thy will be done.'

It will not let you go until you accept the cross, until you pledge yourself to it, until you have learned to say 'Yes, Father', and so cannot fall into despair.

It wants to teach you to humble yourself beneath the hand of God, because you recognise that 'I, a sinner, need this experience'.

It wants to teach you patience. Those who are patient will receive a crown, because they have endured to the end.

It wants to teach you to be meek when you are grieved by torments and hardships, so that you bear them without protest and rebellion.

It wants to teach you not to yearn for comfort and love, but to depend only upon God and to be triumphant over your irritability.

It wants to teach you to believe, even when human help has come to an end, that God is the Master of your body.

It wants to teach you not to think of yourself, but to suffer with others, to give them love and so forget your own suffering.

It wants to teach you the song in the night which brings thanks to God in suffering, because he gives us glory through suffering.

It wants to teach you to thank him for suffering, because it prepares you for glory and brings blessings and joy without end.

It wants to teach you to bring forth the fruit for which God often looks in vain among his children, the fruit which only comes from suffering.

Jesus, my all in all thou art,
My rest in toil, mine ease in pain;
The med'cine of my broken heart;
In war, my peace; in loss, my gain;
My smile beneath the tyrant's frown;
In shame, my glory and my crown:

In want, my plentiful supply;
In weakness, mine almighty power;
In bonds, my perfect liberty;
My light in Satan's darkest hour;
My help and stay whene'er I call;
My life in death; my heaven, my all.

Charles Wesley   1707-88

O God, I turn my thoughts to you, this morning, as the day begins.
You know the changed circumstances we are involved in just now.
You know how loss of health suddenly reminds us of our human
limitations.

We need your guidance;
we need your sustaining strength;
we need the help of others whom you have given us.

Hallow every hour of this day, and keep us continually aware of your
nearness. We believe that your loving purpose is health and
wholeness for each of us, and peace and quiet trust in our home.

Our knowledge is so limited;
our experience is so small;
our faith affected by our physical state.

And what we ask for ourselves, we would ask for others in a like
position; we do not know all their needs — but you do; we are
powerless to do much to help them — but you can do all that they
need. Do that in the name of Christ.   Amen.

Rita Snowden   *When My Visitors Go*

Sickness of mind

My mind and my body may grow weak, but God is my strength
Psalm 73:26 TEV

It is quite untrue and terribly unkind to suppose that Christians who are sometimes anxious have no faith. Sensitive people of so-called highly-strung natures show fear when the somnolent and phlegmatic see no cause for it and can imagine none.

Further, many, like myself, had fears sown in their hearts during childhood, and have never escaped a certain amount of domination by them or found complete release from them. Just as a child, wounded in the body by some accident or ill-treatment, may limp for life, so a child, assaulted by fear in tender childhood and not treated properly, may mentally, or rather emotionally, limp for life. For myself, if nervously exhausted or even overtired, there sometimes leaps upon the spirit a terrifying fear of something I cannot identify. Many know these nameless terrors and many more know the vague malaise of chronic apprehension. They do all they know physically, mentally and spiritually to cope with life, and many act with a bravery as great as that which a battlefield demands. Let no one belittle their faith or doubt their religious sincerity. If some critics had to face what life asks of a neurotic patient, made so, perhaps, by war-wounds in the mind, they would flee the field and escape at least into chronic invalidism.

Those superior people who can always sleep and who say loftily, 'I go to bed to sleep', after our confession of a sleepless night, might sometimes ask themselves if they are paying themselves a compliment. Paul, we may comfort ourselves, confessed to 'many a sleepless night' and knew what it was to tremble with fear and to be depressed. Yet Paul went on praying to be delivered and gave to the world his prescription: 'In nothing be anxious; but in everything by prayer and supplication with thanksgiving let your requests be made known unto God. And the peace of God, which passeth all understanding, shall guard your hearts and your thoughts in Christ Jesus.'

Leslie Weatherhead   *A Private House of Prayer*

Christ the healer

I was a stricken deer, that left the herd
Long since. With many an arrow deep infixt
My panting side was charged, when I
*   withdrew*
To seek a tranquil death in distant shades.
There was I found by One who had himself
Been hurt by th'archers. In his side he bore,
And in his hands and feet, the cruel scars.
With gentle force soliciting the darts,
He drew them forth, and healed, and bade
*   me live.*

William Cowper 1731-1800   from *The Task*

Dear Lord Jesus, give me strength which I now need, the strength to
endure suffering. I open my sad heart to you so that you can fill me
with your love. I surrender myself to follow in your footsteps along
the way of the cross — the way you are now leading me.
Your love always sends help to me, your weak child. My Father, you
love me, you will carry me through in your strong arms. I rest
trustingly and quietly in your heart. I am your child, my Father, and
you feel such fatherly love for me. Yes, you are my Father!   Amen.

Basilea Schlink   *The Blessings of Illness*

Caring for others

Bear one another's burdens, and so fulfil the law of Christ.
Galatians 6:2 RSV

Life had been particularly hectic for the disciples. They had just returned from an exciting and exhausting mission of healing and preaching, only to find that where the Master was there was so much coming and going that they hadn't even time to eat their meals. Jesus, himself working to capacity, understood their exhaustion and prescribed rest. On arrival at the quiet place they had chosen, they found a huge crowd awaiting the Lord. What would our reaction have been? Irritation? Disappointment? Resentment? A very different response from the Lord's, for when Jesus saw them, 'his heart was touched with pity for them'. He did not see an anonymous and unwelcome crowd, but individual men and women with needs that he could meet. He gave no thought to his own tiredness, to the constant demands made on his strength and patience — all his love and care went out in pity to those with whom he came in contact.

At what point do people cease to be people to us? If we have time, and things are going well, we do try to see things from their point of view, but only too soon the unobliging shop assistant, the person who pushes in front of us in the bus queue, even the members of our own family, cease to be given the consideration due to human beings and represent instead a hindrance to *my* plans, or a waste of *my* valuable time. Every one I come in contact with has problems, difficulties, frustrations, needs as great or greater than mine. Can I learn from the Master to see each one as a person and, forgetting self, meet their needs, with his help, in courtesy and love?

> *I thought Love lived in the hot sunshine,*
> *But O he lives in the moony light!*
> *I thought to find Love in the heat of the day,*
> *But sweet Love is the comforter of night.*
>
> *Seek Love in the pity of other's woe,*
> *In the gentle relief of another's care,*
> *In the darkness of night and the winter's snow,*
> *In the naked and outcast, seek Love there.*

William Blake   1757-1827

108

How can we care for Grandma, Lord?

Heavenly Father, Grandma is not well.
   She is not able to sleep comfortably
   and her eyesight impairs her ability to cook for herself.
     She needs help and care.

We have spent several weekend afternoons
   driving to homes —
   nursing homes,
   rest homes —
     to find a place where she can stay.

I ask myself if we should have her come to live with us.
What is the right thing to do?
   What is the meaning of responsibility?
   Who should care for the ageing?
   Am I pushing my responsibility away
or is nursing-home care truly better for her now?

We dearly love her.
Is love measured in time or
   in efficiency,
   in proximity,
     or in a familiar environment?
Or is love more profound than that?

Is it more loving to find her another home, away from us?
I am afraid she will feel hurt and rejected if we put her in an
institution.
I dread her reaction — perhaps she won't accept this change.

Whom do I consider first —
   my parents,
   my husband,
   my children,
   myself?
You know what is best.
   Lead us to those who can help us decide.
   Lead us to the acceptance
     of whatever decision we make.
     Lead us, Lord.

           Judith Mattison   *Prayers from a Mother's Heart*

When trouble comes

Endure what you suffer as being a father's punishment; your suffering shows that God is treating you as his sons . . . Later, however, those who have been disciplined by such punishment reap the peaceful reward of a righteous life.

Hebrews 12:7 TEV

My own experience is something like this. I am progressing along the path of life in my ordinary contentedly fallen and godless condition, absorbed in a merry meeting with my friends for the morrow or a bit of work that tickles my vanity today, a holiday or a new book, when suddenly a stab of abdominal pain that threatens serious disease, or a headline in the newspapers that threatens us all with destruction, sends this whole pack of cards tumbling down. At first I am overwhelmed, and all my little happinesses look like broken toys. Then, slowly and reluctantly, bit by bit, I try to bring myself into the frame of mind that I should be in at all times. I remind myself that all these toys were never intended to possess my heart, that my true good is in another world and my only real treasure is Christ. And perhaps, by God's grace, I succeed, and for a day or two become a creature consciously dependent on God and drawing its strength from the right sources. But the moment the threat is withdrawn, my whole nature leaps back to the toys: I am even anxious, God forgive me, to banish from my mind the only thing that supported me under the threat because it is now associated with the misery of those few days. Thus the terrible necessity of tribulation is only too clear. God has had me for but forty-eight hours and then only by dint of taking everything else away from me. Let him but sheathe that sword for a moment and I behave like a puppy when the hated bath is over — I shake myself as dry as I can and race off to reacquire my comfortable dirtiness, if not in the nearest manure heap, at least in the nearest flower bed. And that is why tribulations cannot ease until God either sees us remade or sees that our remaking is now hopeless.

C S Lewis   *The Problem of Pain*

I have no wit, no words, no tears;
    My heart within me like a stone
Is numbed too much for hopes or fears;
    Look right, look left, I dwell alone;
I lift mine eyes, but dimmed with grief
    No everlasting hills I see;
My life is in the falling leaf:
    O Jesus, quicken me.

My life is like a faded leaf,
    My harvest dwindled to a husk;
Truly my life is void and brief
    And tedious in the barren dusk;
My life is like a frozen thing,
    No bud nor greenness can I see:
Yet rise it shall — the sap of Spring;
    O Jesus, rise in me.

My life is like a broken bowl,
    A broken bowl that cannot hold
One drop of water for my soul
    Or cordial in the searching cold;
Cast in the fire the perished thing,
    Melt and remould it, till it be
A royal cup for him my King:
    O Jesus, drink of me.

Christina Rossetti   1830-94

Father, you have promised to be with your children in the midst of trouble. Help me to know by faith that you love me and care about me and that you are not far away as you seem to be. You are with me in all I am suffering.

You have promised too to use troubles to make us more like our Lord and Master.

I want to accept what has come into my life as something you can transform and bless. I give myself and my circumstances into your hands. Bring good out of this evil for your glory. In Jesus' name.   Amen.

When I am worried

I will climb my watch-tower and wait to see what the Lord will tell me to say and what answer he will give to my complaint.

Habakkuk 2:1 TEV

If you take your problem to God, leave it with God. You have no right to brood over it any longer. In his perplexity, Habakkuk says, 'I am going to get out of this vale of depression; I am going to the watch-tower; I am going up to the heights; I am going to look to God and to God alone' — one of the most important secrets of the Christian life! If you have committed your problem to God and go on thinking about it, it means that your prayers were not genuine.

If you told God on your knees that you had reached an impasse, and that you could not solve your problem, and that you were handing it over to him, then leave it with him. Resolutely refuse to think about it or talk about it. Do not go to the first Christian you meet and say, 'You know, I have an awful problem; I don't know what to do.' Don't discuss it. Leave it with God, and go on to the watch-tower. This may not be easy for us. We may have to be almost violent in forcing ourselves to do this. It is none the less essential. We must never allow ourselves to become submerged by a difficulty, to be shut in by the problem. We must come right out of it — 'I will stand upon my watch, and set me upon the tower.' We have to extricate ourselves deliberately, to haul ourselves out of it, as it were, to detach ourselves from it altogether, and then take our stand looking to God — not at the problem.

Martyn Lloyd-Jones   *From Fear To Faith*

> *Leave God to order all thy ways,*
> *And hope in him whate'er betide;*
> *Thou'lt find him in the evil days*
> *Thy all-sufficient strength and guide:*
> *Who trusts in God's unchanging love*
> *Builds on the rock that nought can move.*

Georg Christian Neumark 1621-81;
tr. by Catherine Winkworth

I've got to talk to somebody, God.

I'm worried, I feel unhappy. I feel inadequate so often, hopeless, defeated, afraid.

But nobody pauses to listen, out there or here — here in the very house where I live. Even those closest to me are so busy, so absorbed in their own concerns.

They nod and murmur and make an effort to share it, but they can't; I know they can't before I begin.

There are all these walls between us — husband and wife, parent and child, neighbour and neighbour, friend and friend.

Walls of self. Walls of silence. Even walls of words.

For even when we try to talk to each other new walls begin to rise. We camouflage, we hold back, we make ourselves sound better than we really are. Or we are shocked and hurt by what is revealed. Or we sit privately in judgement, criticizing even when we pretend to agree.

But with you, Lord, there are no walls.

You, who made me, know my deepest emotions, my most secret thoughts. You know the good of me and the bad of me, you already understand.

Why, then, do I turn to you?

Because as I talk to you my disappointments are eased, my joys are enhanced. I find solutions to my problems, or the strength to endure what I must.

From your perfect understanding I receive understanding for my own life's needs.

Thank you that I can always turn to you. I've got to talk to somebody, God.

Marjorie Holmes   *Lord, Let Me Love*

Facing the humdrum

Whatever you do, do all to the glory of God.

1 Corinthians 10:31 RSV

In 1666, following his conversion, Brother Lawrence became a lay brother of the Carmelite order in Paris. His work was in the monastery kitchen where he learned, among the pots and pans, to practise the presence of God. In the conversation that follows, he explains how he found God in the humdrum of life:

When he began his business, he said to God, with a filial trust in him: *O my God, since thou art with me, and I must now, in obedience to thy commands, apply my mind to these outward things, I beseech thee to grant me the grace to continue in thy presence; and to this end do thou prosper me with thy assistance, receive all my works, and possess all my affections.*

As he proceeded in his work he continued his familiar conversation with his Maker, imploring his grace, and offering to him all his actions.

When he had finished he examined himself how he had discharged his duty; if he found *well*, he returned thanks to God; if otherwise, he asked pardon, and, without being discouraged, he set his mind right again, and continued his exercise of the *presence* of God as if he had never deviated from it. 'Thus,' said he, 'by rising after my falls, and by frequently renewed acts of faith and love, I am come to a state wherein it would be as difficult for me not to think of God as it was at first to accustom myself to it.'

As Brother Lawrence had found such an advantage in walking in the presence of God, it was natural for him to recommend it earnestly to others; but his example was a stronger inducement than any arguments he could propose. His very countenance was edifying, such a sweet and calm devotion appearing in it as could not but affect the beholders. And it was observed that in the greatest hurry of business in the kitchen he still preserved his recollection and heavenly-mindedness. He was never hasty nor loitering, but did each thing in its season, with an even, uninterrupted composure and tranquillity of spirit. 'The time of business', said he, 'does not with me differ from the time of prayer; and in the noise and clatter of my kitchen, while several persons are at the same time calling for different things, I possess God in as great tranquillity as if I were upon my knees at the blessed sacrament.'

Brother Lawrence   *The Practice of the Presence of God*

New every morning is the love
Our waking and uprising prove;
Through sleep and darkness safely brought,
Restored to life, and power, and thought.

If, on our daily course, our mind
Be set to hallow all we find,
New treasures still of countless price
God will provide for sacrifice.

The trivial round, the common task,
Will furnish all we ought to ask:
Room to deny ourselves; a road
To bring us daily nearer God.

John Keble   1792-1866

Lord Jesus, nearly all your life was spent in a small, uneventful village, working as a craftsman and looking after the family. There was very little excitement and not much chance to 'shine' or take part in stimulating conversations.

This was the kind of situation in which you practised the presence of your Father. You showed what he is like by the care with which you made each yoke and each cradle; by the way you listened to others' sorrows, by the willingness with which you cooked breakfast or tea for the family.

Help me to come to terms with the humdrum kind of life you have appointed for me. Help me to speak to you often and come to know you better. Help me to show your love in the way I do the routine jobs and serve others.

Give me your peace in accepting my life to your glory.   Amen.

Lord of all pots and pans and things . . .
Make me a saint by getting meals
And washing up the plates!
(?)

Living alone

I will be with you always.

Matthew 28:20 TEV

I've just come from visiting a big noisy family and I'm exhausted. Filled with happy memories yes, but glad to get home.

And now seems a good time to realise that instead of lamenting my loneliness, I should be singing the blessings of solitude!

Thank you for silence, Lord. Sheer silence can indeed be golden. And so can order. I gaze about this apartment with new respect; it seems beautiful right now, and simple to keep it so with nobody to pick up after but myself.

And independence — how divine. The freedom to do what I please.

I can listen to the kind of music or watch the kind of television shows I really enjoy. I can read, write, sew, paint or just think without being interrupted.

I can read in bed at night as late as I want without disturbing anybody. I don't have to worry about anybody else's feelings, or have my own unexpectedly hurt. I don't have to argue or pretend to agree when I don't.

I don't have to be bored. I can give a party. I can call up a friend for lunch.

And even if all the people I know are busy, I have only to dial a few numbers, travel a few blocks to be in the thick of those who'll welcome me with open arms. My club, my church — hospitals, the Salvation Army.

More places than I can count, where there are always vital, joyous, stimulating people; and people whose loneliness and needs so far surpass mine that I feel richly endowed and aglow.

Lord, let me remember all this when loneliness gets me down.

And let me remember it also when I get too enamoured with solitude. Don't let me become ingrown and selfish.

There is so much work to be done and so many people to be helped and enjoyed. Especially for the woman who lives alone.

Margaret Evening   *Who Walk Alone*

I will look above the high risers.
If I wants to find some help,
It comes from God who made everything.

He won't let you get pushed around.
He won't go to sleep on you
And he will always be interested in you.

God is the kind of father
That you wished you had.

No one can sneak up on you when he is around
Either in the day or in the night
Or when the street light's busted.

He will keep the big kids
From beatin' on you,
And they won't hurt you with him around.

God watches over you
Every place you go
And for all your life.

(Psalm 121 interpreted for today by an inner-city boy)
Carl Burke   *God is For Real, Man*

God be in my head, and in my understanding;
God be in mine eyes, and in my looking;
God be in my mouth, and in my speaking;
God be in my heart, and in my thinking;
God be at my end, and at my departing.

Book of Hours   1514

When I need guidance

The Lord says, 'I will teach you the way you should go; I will instruct you and advise you. Don't be stupid like a horse or a mule, which must be controlled with a bit and bridle to make it submit.'

Psalm 32:8-9 TEV

But how then may the Lord's guidance be expected? After what has been premised negatively, the question may be answered in a few words. In general, he guides and directs his people, by affording them, in answer to prayer, the light of his Holy Spirit, which enables them to understand and to love the Scriptures. The word of God is not to be used as a lottery; nor is it designed to instruct us by shreds and scraps, which, detached from their proper places, have no determinate import; but it is to furnish us with just principles, right apprehensions to regulate our judgements and affections, and thereby to influence and direct our conduct. They who study the Scriptures, in an humble dependence upon divine teaching, are convinced of their own weakness, are taught to make a true estimate of everything around them, are gradually formed into a spirit of submission to the will of God, discover the nature and duties of their several situations and relations in life, and the snares and temptations to which they are exposed. The word of God dwells richly in them, is a preservative from error, a light to their feet, and a spring of strength and consolation. By treasuring up the doctrines, precepts, promises, examples, and exhortations of Scripture, in their minds, and daily comparing themselves with the rule by which they walk, they grow into an habitual frame of spiritual wisdom, and acquire a gracious taste, which enables them to judge of right and wrong with a degree of readiness and certainty, as a musical ear judges of sounds. And they are seldom mistaken, because they are influenced by the love of Christ, which rules in their hearts, and a regard to the glory of God, which is the great object they have in view.

John Newton   *Select Letters*

Thy way, not mine, O Lord,
However dark it be!
Lead me by thine own hand,
Choose out the path for me.

Smooth let it be or rough,
It will be still the best;
Winding or straight, it leads
Right onward to thy rest.

I dare not choose my lot;
I would not, if I might;
Choose thou for me, my God;
So shall I walk aright.

The kingdom that I seek
Is thine; so let the way
That leads to it be thine;
Else I must surely stray.

Not mine, not mine the choice,
In things or great or small;
Be thou my guide, my strength,
My wisdom, and my all!

Horatius Bonar   1808-89

Lord, now, when the future is dark and the next step uncertain, strengthen my faith in you. I take for myself your promises to guide your children. I believe that you will show me the right decision to make, the right action to take.

Help me to be willing, deep down, to go the way of your choosing. Help me not to be swayed by my own preferences or ambitions.

Give me confidence to know that you will not let me make a mistake and wander from your will.

I believe that your way is best for me and for those I love. Guide me into it. For Jesus' sake.   Amen.

When loved ones are away

I thank my God every time I remember you. In all my prayers for all of you, I always pray with joy.

Philippians 1:3-4 NIV

Nothing can fill the gap when we are away from those we love, and it would be wrong to try and find anything. We must simply hold out and win through. That sounds very hard at first, but at the same time it is a great consolation, since leaving the gap unfilled preserves the bonds between us. It is nonsense to say that God fills the gap: he does not fill it, but keeps it empty so that our communion with another may be kept alive, even at the cost of pain. In the second place the dearer and richer our memories, the more difficult the separation. But gratitude converts the pangs of memory into a tranquil joy. The beauties of the past are not endured as a thorn in the flesh, but as a gift precious for its own sake. We must not wallow in our memories or surrender to them, just as we don't gaze all the time at a valuable present, but get it out from time to time, and for the rest hide it away as a treasure we know is there all the time. Treated in this way, the past can give us lasting joy and inspiration. Thirdly, times of separation are not a total loss, nor are they completely unprofitable for our companionship — at least there is no reason why they should be. In spite of all the difficulties they bring, they can be a wonderful means of strengthening and deepening fellowship. Fourthly, it has been borne in upon me here with peculiar force that a concrete situation can always be mastered, and that only fear and anxiety magnify them to an immeasurable degree beforehand. From the moment we awake until we fall asleep we must commend other people wholly and unreservedly to God and leave them in his hands, transforming our anxiety for them into prayers on their behalf.

Dietrich Bonhoeffer   *Letters and Papers from Prison*

Holy Father, in your mercy,
Hear our earnest prayer,
Keep our loved ones, now far distant,
'Neath your care.

Jesus, Saviour, let your presence
Be their light and guide;
Keep, O keep them, in their weakness,
At your side.

When in sorrow, when in danger,
When in loneliness,
In your love look down and comfort
Their distress.

May the joy of your salvation
Be their strength and stay;
May they love and may they praise you
Day by day.

Isabel Stephana Stevenson   1843-90

Lord, it is difficult to face the fact that our children are grown up and that
  our home is no longer
  their home.
Help me not to dwell on my loss but to count the gain.
  Thank you for the happy years when they were young and for the
  memories we can enjoy.
  Thank you that they have reached the maturity and the
  independence for which we trained them.
  Thank you for their visits
    their letters,
    their phone calls.
  Help me never to be possessive,
    interfering,
    demanding,
  always dwelling nostalgically on the past.
  Help me not only to enjoy my memories but to build up a new
  relationship with them which will enrich the present.   Amen.

When I need patience

You need to be patient, in order to do the will of God and receive what he promises.

Hebrews 10:36 TEV

When I was a boy I used to like the story of Joseph. I used to think what fun it must have been to be Joseph — all those adventures and the big success story it all turned into. Now that I am much older and have spent a good many years working with people and so often with people in trouble, this story about Joseph has lost all that fun-and-adventure touch. When I now come to this part where Joseph is just forgotten — forgotten even by the lucky butler who was so glad to have his head still on his shoulders that he could just forget Joseph — then I must confess it puts quite a lump in my throat, and I am not ashamed to admit that I take off my slightly misty bifocals and give them a good polishing. Because this seems to me to be the part of the story that is nearly impossible to follow. Couldn't God have made the butler remember Joseph? Of course he could. Then did God intend deliberately that Joseph was to be left there day after day, month after month, two long tragic further years, before he would make another move?

Yes, this is the way God does it. This is his plan in love. The truth of the matter is that God is the only One who does remember Joseph. Jacob remembers him only to mourn for him. His brothers remember him only to chuckle quietly (when Dad can't hear them) and refer occasionally to 'twenty pieces of silver' as if it were a family joke. Potiphar remembers him only because he now has to try to look after his own affairs. Mrs. Potiphar remembers him only in the growing bitterness of dislike for Captain Potiphar. And the butler doesn't remember him at all.

But God remembers him, every day, all the day. 'God was with him, showing him steadfast love.' Let us go on, seeing his love at work.

John Hercus   *Pages from God's Casebook*

Be still, my soul: the Lord is on thy side;
Bear patiently the cross of grief or pain;
Leave to thy God to order and provide;
In every change he faithful will remain.
Be still, my soul: thy best, thy heavenly
*   Friend*
Through thorny ways leads to a joyful end.

Be still, my soul: thy God doth undertake
To guide the future as he has the past.
Thy hope, thy confidence let nothing shake;
All now mysterious shall be bright at last.
Be still, my soul: the waves and winds still
*   know*
His voice who ruled them while he dwelt
*   below.*

Katharine Von Schlegel,   b.1697
tr. Jane Laurie Borthwick   1813-97

Lord, you are never in a hurry and I always am. I want quick results.
I want to see the end before I begin. Please teach me this most
difficult lesson of patience.
Help me to be patient with other people —
    with my own family,
    with the neighbours,
    with the elderly,
Help me to be patient with myself. I so often make the same
mistakes. Thank you for your patience and forgiveness. Make me
willing to forgive myself and start again.
Give me patience in difficult circumstances.
It seems as if you have forgotten me or let things get out of control.
But I believe that you are still at work, ordering and planning for my
good.
My times are in your hand. Thank you, Father.   Amen.

When I am successful

Beware lest you say in your heart, 'My power and the might of my hand have gotten me this wealth.'
Deuteronomy 8:17 RSV
Not to us, O Lord, not to us, but to thy name give glory.
Psalm 115:1 RSV

How *do* you handle success? Opportunity would be a fine thing, you might retort. But the sweet taste of success comes to most of us at some stage of life. A little money — a little fame — either in our own right or through the family. The question is: how to accept and use it gracefully. A word of caution. Even our best friends may not be over the moon at our success. Most find it a good deal easier to mourn with those who mourn than to rejoice with those who rejoice. So keep a low profile.

Understandably the Bible has more to say to those in trouble than to those riding high. But there is advice for times of success which can help us keep our feet on the ground. Accept your success as a gift from God, Moses reminded Israel. Don't take the credit for it yourself. Even if your skills or hard work have achieved it, these are God-given. And don't give yourself a pat on the back and think what a good sort you must be for God to bless you, Moses added. Look back a minute and call to mind all those past failures and sins and then you'll realize that your present success is all of God's goodness and grace. Since success comes from God it is to be used for him. Money, skills, influence, all bring opportunities that others do not have. We are to be worthy of God's trust and capitalize on every asset for his kingdom.

Most important of all, recognize God's standard of success. Jesus reminded his followers that to be the greatest in his kingdom a person must choose the lowest place. A friend passed on a story about a mutual friend who was serving a term of office as principal of a theological college in India. He was a brilliant young Australian, now a bishop in the church. Owing to a dispute, the college lavatories had been left uncleaned. None of the students would demean himself by doing such a job — reserved in India for the lowest in society. What was their amazement and shame to come upon their own principal, with another visiting lecturer, cleaning their toilets himself! He achieved success in the kingdom not by his intellect or his status but by willingly becoming servant of all.

Be thou my Vision, O Lord of my heart;
Naught be all else to me, save that thou art;
Thou my best thought, by day or by night,
Waking or sleeping, thy presence my light.

Riches I need not, nor man's empty praise,
Thou mine inheritance, now and always:
Thou and thou only, first in my heart,
High King of heaven, my treasure thou art.

High King of heaven, after victory won,
May I reach heaven's joys, O bright heaven's Sun!
Heart of my own heart, whatever befall,
Still be my Vision, O Ruler of all.

Ancient Irish

Lord, you have said, 'Let not the wise man glory in his wisdom, let not the mighty man glory in his might, let not the rich man glory in his riches; but let him who glories glory in this, that he understands and know me.'

Please rescue me from the danger of taking credit for any kind of success that may come my way. Keep me humble, serving others. Help me to set the course of my life so that it may bring credit to Jesus Christ our Lord, who is worthy to receive power and wealth and wisdom and might and honour and glory and blessing for ever and ever. Amen.

Loneliness

They all forsook him, and fled.   Mark 14:50 RSV
Jesus cried with a loud voice, 'My God, my God, why hast thou forsaken me?'   Mark 15:34 RSV

Yes, I do at times feel lonely. Terribly lonely. Yet somehow I know that out of loneliness, if you can face it, and if you can renounce self-pity, and if you can overcome the great urge to blame other people, then there can come a strange but wonderful experience of being alone.

You don't love other people less. In true aloneness you love them more. You stand alone and out of the freedom that you now have you can give without needing a return. You never strike a bargain like 'If you love me then I will love you'. You simply say, 'I love you whether you love me or not.' Of course you can't do it all the time. Only Jesus could and can do that. Of course it hurts when having loved you get smashed in the teeth as your reward, and you are tempted to say, 'Never again'. By and large, though, because you have learned to be alone, your need to be loved by other human beings lessens. I still need Jesus though and always will. He went all the way alone, and because he could go all the way, he can love you as no other person will ever be able to.

I still need him. I don't know why this should be. It is the way that God the Creator made us. To go into aloneness without Jesus could drive a person mad and even to suicide.

Don't seek aloneness unless you enter that with him. He could take it, you can't. I have known people who have gone into loneliness and on into aloneness without him, and as far as this life is concerned, 'they' have ceased to exist, even though their bodies have stayed alive.

However, with him, it is in aloneness that the real treasures lie. You will find him in a way that otherwise you would not. You will love in a way that otherwise you could not. You will find what it is to be a real human being. I have only started the journey but I know the path, and I know that following it is what being alive is all about.

Roy Trevivian   *So You're Lonely*

Tonight, Lord, I am alone.
Little by little the sounds died down in the church,
The people went away,
And I came home,
Alone.

Here I am, Lord,
Alone.
The silence troubles me,
The solitude oppresses me.

Son, you are not alone,
I am with you,
I am you.

I need your hands to continue to bless,
I need your lips to continue to speak,
I need your body to continue to suffer,
I need your heart to continue to love,
I need you to continue to save,
Stay with me, son.

Here I am, Lord;
Here is my body,
Here is my heart,
Here is my soul.
Grant that I may be big enough to reach the world,
Strong enough to carry it,
Pure enough to embrace it without wanting to keep it.

Lord, tonight, while all is still and I feel sharply the sting of solitude,
While the whole world presses on my shoulders with all its weight of
misery and sin.
I repeat to you my 'yes' — not in a burst of laughter, but slowly,
clearly, humbly.
Alone, Lord, before you,
In the peace of the evening.

Michel Quoist   *Prayers of Life*

Thankfulness

Rejoice always, pray constantly, give thanks in all circumstances; for this is the will of God in Christ Jesus for you.

1 Thessalonians 5:16-18 RSV

On either side doors opened into two still larger rooms. Betsie and I followed a prisoner-guide through the door at the right. We followed our guide single file. At last she pointed to a second tier in the centre of a large block. To reach it we had to stand on the bottom level, haul ourselves up, and then crawl across three other straw-covered platforms to reach the one that we would share with — how many? We lay back, struggling against the nausea that swept over us from the reeking straw.

Suddenly I sat up, striking my head on the cross-slats above. Something had pinched my leg.

'Fleas!' I cried. 'Here! And here another one!' I wailed. 'Betsie, how can we live in such a place!'

'Show us, Show us how.' It was said so matter of factly it took me a second to realize she was praying.

'Corrie!' she said excitedly. 'He's given us the answer! In the Bible this morning. Read that part again!'

I glanced down the long dim aisle to make sure no guard was in sight, then drew the Bible from its pouch. 'It was in 1 Thessalonians,' I said. 'Rejoice always, pray constantly, give thanks in all circumstances; for this is the will of God in Christ Jesus.'

'That's it, Corrie! That's his answer. "Give thanks in all circumstances." That's what we can do. We can start right now to thank God for every single thing about this new barracks.'

*   *   *

'Thank you,' Betsie went on serenely, 'for the fleas and for —'

The fleas! This was too much. 'Betsie, there's no way even God can make me grateful for a flea.'

' "Give thanks in *all* circumstances",' she quoted. 'It doesn't say in pleasant circumstances. Fleas are part of this place where God has put us.'

And so we stood between tiers of bunks and gave thanks for fleas. But this time I was sure Betsie was wrong.

Corrie Ten Boom   *The Hiding Place*

Every evening after this Betsie and Corrie held meetings in their crowded dormitory. Women of all nationalities joined to worship and sing, to pray and listen to the Bible. The evenings were 'little previews of heaven'. One thing only puzzled them. Why did no guards come near, no camp police break up their meetings? It was some time later that they discovered the answer. No guard or police would cross the threshold of *those* dormitories — because of the fleas!

Fill thou my life, O Lord my God,
In every part with praise,
That my whole being may proclaim
Thy being and thy ways.

Not for the lip of praise alone,
Nor e'en the praising heart,
I ask, but for a life made up
Of praise in every part.

Praise in the common things of life,
Its goings out and in;
Praise in each duty and each deed,
However small and mean.

Fill every part of me with praise;
Let all my being speak
Of thee and of thy love, O lord,
Poor though I be and weak.

Horatius Bonar   1808-89

Lord, my heart is full of thankfulness today for your love and for the good things you have given me. Accept my thanks.
Teach me to praise you too on days when I feel like grumbling. Make me thankful when circumstances might make me downhearted. For this is the will of God in Christ Jesus for me.   Amen.

Depression

Why am I so sad?
Why am I so troubled?
I will put my hope in God, and once again I will praise him, my
saviour and my God.   Psalm 43:5 TEV

I remember listening to an edition of Woman's Hour where various
speakers described their personal remedies for a fit of the blues. One
took to gardening, another to tidying cupboards while a third wrote
letters to friends in worse plight than herself. I wondered how far
these personal antidotes would help others of different
temperament. The worst of trying to follow good advice and finding
it doesn't work is that the sufferer is left even more depressed —
there is the added ingredient of guilt. Counting blessings or thinking
of others worse off just does not always help, which makes me — as
a Christian — ashamed and more miserable.

I must stress at this point that I am not writing about the kind of
depression which is an illness requiring medical attention but about
the occasional sense of bleakness and gloom that attacks most
women who are coping with the stress of modern living at less than
full health or strength.

I am too old a hand at being depressed to try to pass on my
particular tip in the hope that it would meet others' needs. But there
is one first step which is I believe of value to everyone. The psalmist
said, 'Out of the depths I cry to thee, O Lord' (Ps. 130:1). That
phrase, 'out of the depths' expresses perfectly the sensation of
hopelessness, distance and blackness we experience at such times.
We can't cheer ourselves up, we can't feel God is near or even make
a move towards him. We may feel tempted to put off prayer until
God seems more real. But like the psalmist we *can* cry to God out of
our particular depth. Having cast ourselves honestly, in all our need
on his mercy we can endure the blackness and despair until in due
course he answers, as he always does. One way or another he will
show us his tender love and compassion in the small happenings and
details of life and with a renewed sense of being loved and cared for
our cloud will pass and the sun come out again.

In heavenly love abiding,
No change my heart shall fear;
And safe is such confiding,
For nothing changes here:
The storm may roar without me,
My heart may low be laid;
But God is round about me,
And can I be dismayed?

Green pastures are before me
Which yet I have not seen;
Bright skies will soon be o'er me,
Where the dark clouds have been:
My hope I cannot measure,
My path to life is free;
My Saviour has my treasure,
And he will walk with me.

Anna Laetitia Waring

Lord Jesus Christ, you have promised that whoever follows you shall
not walk in darkness but shall have the light of life. Shed your light
today on hearts that are darkened by despair and depression. Help
us to say with confidence: 'When I sit in darkness the Lord shall be a
light, unto me,' and to go forward trusting you.   Amen.

Anger

You must put to death, then, the earthly desires at work in you . . . you must get rid of all these things: anger, passions and hateful feelings . . . for you have taken off the old self with its habits and have put on the new self. Colossians 3:5, 8, 9, 10 TEV

The Holy Spirit can develop his fruits in our lives if we want this to happen. But the only way we can show that we want the fruits of the Spirit is to attempt to put on the qualities of Christ. We are not expected to sit around, do nothing, and expect the fruits of the Spirit to sprout out of our ears.

Having said all this, however, we are still left with the problem of those residual aggressions fighting to get out. Does putting them to death mean that we pretend they don't exist? I think not. It means that we dispose of them in an area where they cannot harm anybody, not even the cat! There is only one way to do that and it is a way that relatively few Christians seem to have realized. We are meant to pour out our anger *towards God himself!* This is what David did. It is what Jeremiah did. There is abundant evidence of it in the Bible and yet so many of us feel that our prayers should always be processed into a religious type of politeness.

I confess that I rarely have the good sense to follow the example of King David. If I have been involved in a painful clash with someone where I have returned soft answers to constant abuse the likelihood is that next time I have the car to myself I shall spit the real feelings on my mind towards the windscreen wipers. This is certainly better than doing it towards the person in question but the problem is that it tends only to reinforce the resentment I feel at being abused. No — the true way is to tell God exactly what I feel. He knows anyway! If I feel that God shouldn't have allowed me to be so treated I might as well say it and have the relief from getting it out of my system. He is already aware that I feel that way so I might as well be honest.

Things like a hard dig in the garden (one of my wife's great ploys) or a vigorous walk all help — but to let it all come out before our understanding and unshockable heavenly Father is still the best way.

Gavin Reid *A New Happiness*

Lord, I saw the sea attacking the rocks, sombre and raging.
From afar the waves gained momentum.
High and proud, they leapt, jostling one another to be the first
    to strike.
When the white foam drew back, leaving the rock clear, they
    gathered themselves to rush forward again.

The other day I saw the sea, calm and serene.
The waves came from afar, creeping, not to draw attention.
Quietly holding hands, they slipped noiselessly and stretched at
    full length on the sand, to touch the shore with the tips
    of their beautiful, soft fingers.
The sun gently caressed them, and they generously returned
    streams of light.

Lord, grant that I may avoid useless quarrels that tire and
    wound without achieving results.
Keep me from those angry outbursts that draw attention but
    leave one uselessly weakened.
Keep me from wanting always to outstrip others in my conceit,
    crushing those in my way.
Wipe from my face the look of dark, dominating anger.
Rather, Lord, grant that I may live my days calmly and fully, as
    the sea slowly covers the whole shore.
Make me humble like the sea, as, silently and gently, it spreads
    out, unnoticed.
May I wait for my brothers and match my pace to theirs, that I
    may move upward with them.

Grant me the triumphant perseverance of the waters.
May each of my retreats turn into an advance.
Give my face the light of clear waters.
Give my soul the whiteness of foam.
Illumine my life that it may sing like sunbeams on the surface of
    the sea.
But above all, Lord, may I not keep this light for myself, and
    may all those who come near me return home eager
    to bathe in your eternal grace.

Michel Quoist   *Prayers of Life*

Jealousy

Peace of mind makes the body healthy, but jealousy is like a cancer.
Proverbs 14:30 TEV

'She really shouldn't wear pink at her age,' we remark. What we *mean* is 'Why should she have another outfit when I can't afford anything new?' But we are so ashamed of jealousy that we often disguise it well enough to deceive ourselves as well as others. Yet deep down we are jealous not only of others' possessions but of their gifts and personalities too. Why can't *I* have a house full of visitors and stay calm and collected? Why am I never able to think of the right thing to say like she does? If only I could organize like her!

It may console us to know that most people suffer pangs of envy. Others' talents and circumstances look so much more congenial than our own. Even Shakespeare wrote:

> Wishing me like to one more rich in hope,
> Featur'd like him, like him with friends possessed,
> Desiring this man's art or that man's scope.

Jealousy springs from dissatisfaction with ourselves and our lot. It is right to regret our failures and hate our sin. It is not right to hate or despise the self that God has given. In his infinite variety he has chosen to make each unique. Quiet or talkative, quick of mind, nimble-fingered, he wants to recreate us in Christ using *that* raw material and not any other. When we envy others it may mean that we are unwilling to accept God's blueprint in creating us.

The corresponding virtue which the ancient writers set alongside envy was love. First we must learn to love God so that we accept the self that he has made without constantly throwing it back in his face. Unlikely material it may seem, but he can make something useful and lovely from it. Next we must learn to love ourselves. To love means to accept — with all the limitations and disadvantages attached. When we have learned these kinds of loving we shall not need to be jealous of others. We can accept and love them too, loving our neighbour as ourselves, because we love God. And love envies not.

Lord, something rather serious; big.
You have a minute or two?
It may take more, but the subject will be familiar to you
    and you may have a ready-mixed cure.
It's jealousy, Lord.
Familiar? Cain and Abel? Joseph? Jacob?
    And all the millions since then?

Well, Lord, for a person to know he's one of millions,
    alive and dead, is no help at all. None.
Jealousy narrows a person, Lord.
    Makes his soul smaller; his character meaner.
    Makes him cutting in his words, without trust.
Full of suspicion and very dark thoughts.

Need we have it, Lord? What good does it do?
    It proves nothing — and demands much.
    It breeds violence — and creates fear.
It shrivels a person, Lord, makes him less.
It sits on his shoulder like a vulture covered in green
    slime, murmuring lies and obscenities, with bad
    breath.
Who needs it, Lord?

David Kossoff   *You Have a Minute, Lord?*

Lord, I need you to deal with the jealousy in my life. Sometimes it is
a nagging pain that takes away peace of mind and stops me being
useful to you. Sometimes it is so sharp and fierce that it takes over
my whole thinking and stops my prayers. Only you can deal with this
cancer of jealousy. I want to be free of it. I put myself in your hands.
Give me your love in place of my envy. For Jesus' sake.   Amen.

Guilt

If we confess our sins, he is faithful and just, and will forgive our sins and cleanse us from all unrighteousness.   1 John 1:9 RSV

A whole book could be written about why people feel guilty and why a lot of the guilt is unnecessary. On the other hand some people have every reason to feel guilty and they need the forgiveness of God.

It is not by chance that at the heart of the Christian message Jesus called (and calls) for people everywhere to repent and accept forgiveness. It is obvious to me that Jesus knew that eating at the heart of every human being like a cancer lies a burden of guilt, which can be healed by the word of forgiveness.

'Forgive us our trespasses as we forgive those who trespass against us,' says the Lord's Prayer, 'Neither do I condemn you,' said Jesus. 'Go and sin no more,' he said to the woman who had committed adultery.

Stay within the isolation of your guilt if that is what you choose. Present a guilt-free face to the world if you can't trust in forgiveness, and let the cancer of secret guilt eat away at your soul.

But neither should we parade our guilt and wallow in it publicly. That is simply obnoxious and infinitely boring.

Just quietly and humbly share your guilt with someone who can accept it and not be damaged by it. Then the prison cell opens and you can walk out into the clean, fresh air, free, free to love and free to be loved, with the future offering a new beginning.

At the heart of the Christian Gospel is the cross. That cross is God's way of saying that if you are truly and honestly sorry for what you have done wrong, then forgiveness and freedom from guilt are yours. It puzzles me why so many people ignore this priceless gift.

It is also strange that so many people who know that the gospel is about forgiveness just cannot believe that such forgiveness is for them. John Bunyan and John Wesley were both plagued with the conviction that they could not be forgiven. When at last the realization that they were forgiven entered their tortured minds, they became new men with a gospel of liberation for tens of thousands of people.

Roy Trevivian   *So You're Lonely*

Love bade me welcome; yet my soul drew back,
    Guilty of dust and sin.
But quick-eyed love, observing me grow slack
    From my first entrance in,
Drew nearer to me, sweetly questioning
    If I lacked anything.

'A guest,' I answered, 'worthy to be here.'
    Love said, 'You shall be he.'
'I, the unkind, ungrateful? Ah, my dear,
    I cannot look on thee.'
Love took my hand and smiling did reply,
    'Who made the eyes but I?'

'Truth, Lord; but I have marred them: Let my shame
    Go where it doth deserve.'
'And know you not,' says Love, 'who bore the blame?'
    'My dear, then I will serve.'
'You must sit down,' says Love, 'and taste my meat.'
    So I did sit and eat.

George Herbert   1593-1633

Dear Lord Jesus, I cannot forget my sin and guilt. I am truly sorry and I do believe that you carried my sin in your own body on the tree. Help me now to believe with all my heart that you forgive me. Free me from this heavy load of guilt.   Amen.

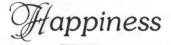

Happiness

Is anyone happy? He should sing praises.   James 5:13 TEV

Some time in the night I awoke, feeling the yacht swinging at her anchor. A stream of lovely cool air was pouring down the forward hatch. I got up soundlessly and emerged from the hatch as far as my waist. At the same instant Davy popped out of the after hatch and crept forward along the deck to where I stood, half out of the hatch. The breeze had sprung up and backed to north so that it was coming straight in the mouth of the cove, though not strongly enough to cause any worry about the anchor holding. It had blown every bit of humidity and sultriness away. The air was cool and fresh. Ten thousand brilliant stars arched across the sky. But what transfixed us was phosphorescence. Every little wave rolling into the cove was crested with cold fire. The anchor rode was a line of fire going down into the depths, and fish moving about left trails of fire. The night of the sea-fire. Davy had crept near to me, still crouching, and I put my arm about her, and she snuggled close. Neither of us spoke, not so much as a whispered word. We were together, we were close, we were overwhelmed by a great beauty. I know that it seemed to us both that we were completely one: we had no *need* to speak. We remained so in timeless loveliness — was it hours? We never knew. All about us was the extraordinary beauty of the sea-fire and the glittering stars overhead. We were full of wonder — and joy. *Grey Goose* was alive, lifting to the little waves, and the tall dark masts were pencilling across the stars. The moment was utterly timeless: we didn't know that time existed; and it contained, therefore, some foretaste, it may be, of eternity. At last, still with no word spoken, we went below again and, in comfort and a great peace, slept.

Sheldon Vanauken   *A Severe Mercy*

Glory be to God for dappled things —
For skies of couple-colour as a brinded cow;
For rose-moles all in stipple upon trout that swim;
Fresh-firecoal chestnut-falls; finches' wings;
Landscape plotted and pieced — fold, fallow, and
plough;
And all trades, their gear and tackle and trim.

All things counter, original, spare, strange;
Whatever is fickle, freckled (who knows how?)
With swift, slow; sweet, sour; adazzle, dim;
He fathers-forth whose beauty is past change:
Praise him.

Gerard Manley Hopkins   *Pied Beauty*

Thank you, Father, for days, hours or moments of happiness that we
enjoy. Our hearts go out in gratitude to you
For the beauty of the world,
for the ecstasy of love,
for the warmth of friendship,
for the delight of small children.
Thank you for laughter, for music,
for pets, for memories,
for a new book or a new dress.
So many things give us happiness — great things and small — and
there are so many kinds of happiness. But we receive it all in
thankfulness from you, our Father.
Bring us at last to the perfect happiness of heaven, for in your
presence is fulness of joy and at your right hand are pleasures for
evermore. Through Jesus Christ our Lord.   Amen.

Fear

Behold, God is my salvation; I will trust, and will not be afraid.
Isaiah 12:2 RSV

I have a feeling that when doubts and anxieties assail us, common sense is the first thing to go. We long for easy answers, unambiguous assurance. The doubts and guilts drown our minds and make us not *want* to think rationally but instead to cling to any bit of ideological driftwood that comes along. The last thing we want to do when we are drowning is to think logically.

Yet think we must.

As a recently graduated doctor I was given major duties in surgery too early.

Understandably, things sometimes went wrong — seriously wrong. In the operating room a wave of panic would occasionally begin to rise in me as with horror I would see that the operation was getting into a deeper and deeper mess. An unconscious patient's life depended on me. The anaesthetist was competent in his or her own area but could offer me no help. Senior surgeons were an hour away. With the panic came a sort of freezing in my brain. My movements were hurried but pointless and repetitive. I would stare at the circle of the eyes of the assisting team, but all eyes would be looking silently back at me.

Under such circumstances the only thing I could do was forcefully to will myself to think slowly and deliberately. I discovered that being a Christian I had been sending up panicky prayers, 'Oh Lord, help! Lord, don't let it go wrong! Lord, don't let me get into a mess! Don't let her die!' They were muttered incantations, not prayer. I had not been aiming at communicating with God but was simply expressing panic in parrot talk.

God of course was merciful. *He* was there. But I saw that *I* had to stop and think. On a spiritual level I had to talk to myself rather than to God. 'God *is* here. He doesn't need to be badgered. He *does* care. Now take it easy. What's my *immediate* aim? What should I do first?'

Slowly, as I did this, a mental clearing came. My mind unfroze and I found myself, if not relaxed, at least able to be deliberate and calm. Slowly, with a sense of growing confidence and relief, I found my way through the difficulties, successfully completing what could have been a tragically botched operation. My mind had been freed to accept new ideas, to remember old principles and to force myself to rely on them and go ahead.

I have no doubt that God's Holy Spirit was behind it all. But what was demanded of me in each little crisis was to force myself to stop the panic spiral and think.

John White   *Parents in Pain*

Put thou thy trust in God,
In duty's path go on;
Walk in his strength with faith and hope,
So shall thy work be done.

Give to the winds thy fears;
Hope, and be undismayed;
God hears thy sighs and counts thy tears;
God shall lift up thy head.

Commit thy ways to him,
Thy works into his hands,
And rest on his unchanging word,
Who heaven and earth commands.

Through waves and clouds and storms
His power will clear thy way:
Wait thou his time; the darkest night
Shall end in brightest day.

John Wesley   1703-91 and others

Lord, I am gripped by fear. Loosen its hold on me. Fix my eyes and thoughts on you instead. Let me realize your greatness, your love and your control over everything that can happen to me or to those I love. Give me calmness instead of panic. Show me how to be still. Clear my thinking and guide me to the next step I should take. For Jesus' sake.   Amen.